THE WORLD'S CLASSICS

SYMPOSIUM

PLATO (c.427–347 BC), Athenian philosopher-dramatist, has had a profound and lasting influence upon Western intellectual tradition. Born into a wealthy and prominent family, he grew up during the conflict between Athens and the Peloponnesian states which engulfed the Greek world from 431 to 404 BC. Following its turbulent aftermath, he was deeply affected by the condemnation and execution of his revered master Socrates (469–399) on charges of irreligion and corrupting the young. In revulsion from political activity, Plato devoted his life to the pursuit of philosophy and to composing memoirs of Socratic enquiry cast in dialogue form. He was strongly influenced by the Pythagorean thinkers of southern Italy and Sicily, which he is said to have visited when he was about 40. Some time after returning to Athens, he founded the Academy, an early ancestor of the modern university, devoted to philosophical and mathematical enquiry, and to the education of future rulers or 'philosopher-kings'. The Academy's most celebrated member was the young Aristotle (384–322), who studied there for the last twenty years of Plato's life. Their works mark the highest peak of philosophical achievement in antiquity, and both continue to rank among the greatest philosophers of all time.

Plato is the earliest Western philosopher from whose output complete works have been preserved. At least twenty-five of his dialogues are extant, ranging from fewer than twenty to more than three hundred pages in length. For their combination of dramatic realism, poetic beauty, intellectual vitality, and emotional power they are unique in Western literature.

ROBIN WATERFIELD was born in 1952. After graduating from Manchester University, he went on to research ancient Greek philosophy at King's College, Cambridge. He has been a university lecturer (at Newcastle upon Tyne and St Andrews), and an editor and publisher. Currently, however, he is a self-employed consultant editor and writer, whose books range from philosophy to children's fiction. He has translated, in particular, a number of Plutarch's essays, Xenophon's Socratic works, and several other dialogues by Plato, including *Republic*.

THE WORLD'S CLASSICS

PLATO
Symposium

Translated by
ROBIN WATERFIELD

Oxford   New York
OXFORD UNIVERSITY PRESS

Oxford University Press, Walton Street, Oxford OX2 6DP

Oxford New York
Athens Auckland Bangkok Bombay
Calcutta Cape Town Dar es Salaam Delhi
Florence Hong Kong Istanbul Karachi
Kuala Lumpur Madras Madrid Melbourne
Mexico City Nairobi Paris Singapore
Taipei Tokyo Toronto

and associated companies in
Berlin Ibadan

Oxford is a trade mark of Oxford University Press

British Library Cataloguing in Publication Data
Data available

Library of Congress Cataloging in Publication Data
Plato.
[Symposium. English]
Symposium / Plato ; translated by Robin Waterfield.
p. cm.—(World's classics)
Includes bibliographical references.
1. Socrates. 2. Love.
I. Waterfield, Robin, 1952- .
II. Title. III. Series.
B385.A5W38 1994 184—dc20 93-566
ISBN 0-19-282908-4

5 7 9 10 8 6 4

Printed in Great Britain by
BPC Paperbacks Ltd.
Aylesbury, Bucks

For Raja and Zorine
with thanks for the greatest gift of all

For Pata and Zorine,
with thanks for the greater part of all

CONTENTS

PREFACE

THE balance between philosophy and literary art varies from one of Plato's dialogues to another. *Symposium* favours artistry more than any other work. My strategy in the translation has been to try to reflect the styles and tones of the work as accurately as possible, which means not underplaying or exaggerating aspects of the original. On the one hand, the translation is not quite of the literal kind which a student of Greek could use as a crib; on the other hand, I have not gratuitously added words (as some translators have) to bring out some feature or other of the original. In all its manifestations, true art is never obvious; therefore, to exaggerate features in this way is to ruin the artistry of the piece and to insult the reader by assuming that he or she will not be sensitive to what Plato is saying.

The philosophy of the dialogue is elusive at times. Conversations at crucial stages with Glyn Davies and then with my wife helped bring some matters into focus. Of course, my debts to my wife Briji on the subject of love go far beyond the occasional conversation. Her coaching of an intellectual's clumsy heart has been as rigorous and generous (and no doubt as frustrating) as Diotima's education of Socrates. This translation is dedicated to her parents, with overwhelming gratitude. I also owe thanks to Peter Kingsley and to Oxford University Press's reader for a number of improvements.

R.A.H.W.

INTRODUCTION

PLATO'S *Symposium* is without a doubt one of the most famous works of literature in the Western world. It is living proof that a great book does not need to be a long book. It is also living proof that a great work of literature does not have to be hard to read: *Symposium* is fun, and should really be read in the first place at a single sitting. Some of the reasons for its greatness are impressed upon a reader simply as he or she reads the book; others can usefully be brought out in an introduction.

As everyone knows, *Symposium* is about love. Actually, it is about *erōs*, which is the Greek word for passionate love and in the context of relations between human beings means primarily 'sexual desire'. Nevertheless, Plato extends the reference of the word a great deal in the course of the work, until the only possible English translation for *erōs* is 'love'—love as the motivating force in all of us.

A great many people are also familiar with the English phrase 'platonic love'. My dictionary defines this as 'love between soul and soul, without sensual desire'. Since this is the meaning of the phrase, and since throughout the 'dialogue' (as all Plato's works are called, even when they involve little dialogue) the passionate, sexual connotations of *erōs* are never overlooked, then it is clear that *Symposium* is not about platonic love. In fact, this phrase arose in Renaissance times out of a radical misunderstanding and watering down of Plato's views on love. Whatever platonic love may be, there is nothing insipid about Platonic love.

There are other attitudes towards love which it is vital to clear out of the way from the start. As a topic, love is not far from being a great unknown to most people. We think of certain feelings that arise, especially in our hearts, as love or as manifestations of love; this may be right, but it does not bring us any closer to understanding love, and as long as we do not understand a subject ourselves, we are prey to external influences.

The main external influence in the West today undoubtedly arises from Christianity. The extent to which Plato's conception of love coincides with or differs from the Christian view would only become clear from a longer comparative study than this Introduction allows (and a less partisan one than has occasionally been written). Nevertheless, the following features of the Christian view must be borne in mind: you should love everyone, and love them for themselves, not for what they can do for you. The ideal is to emulate God's love, which is unconditional: God does not love only a portion of his creatures (for instance, if they are good, or white, or baptized). All I want to do here is remind the reader that this may be no more than one possible view, and that if we find a different view in Plato, that does not automatically make Plato wrong. As a matter of fact, Plato links love closely with desire, and therefore asserts that God cannot love, since he is perfect and is in need of nothing. It is not clear that this is, in its own right, a less elevated view of the Divine than that of Christianity. In any case, we will find that Plato's view (as developed in the speech of Socrates-Diotima) is not so much intended to be a particular view of love as an analysis of all kinds of love. The analysis may fit Christian love as well as any other kind.

Other external influences reach us through contemporary literature, theatre, and film, but arguably stem from the medieval Courtly Love writings (as exemplified by the original Arthurian romances) and from Romanticism. The first gives us our tendency to over-invest in the object of our affection—to put him or her on a pedestal (and then later to be disappointed by his or her humanity); the second gives us our tendency to think that in matters of love the heart should be trusted more than the head, and even that the head is positively to be ignored. Again, the reader should watch out for these conditioned ideas and resist the temptation to impose them on Plato or to judge Plato by their standards.

Symposia

In *Symposium* Plato affords us a glimpse of certain aspects of ancient Athenian life which may be somewhat alien to us. The setting is a symposium hosted by the dramatist Agathon in the winter of 416 BC, just after his very first play has carried off the first prize at one of the two main Athenian dramatic festivals. Both the host and the guests are gentlemen of leisure: they may have occupations, but they do not need to work for a living.

Following Socrates' death, a number of his admirers began to write pieces with Socrates as the protagonist. Curiously, one of the works of Xenophon, the only other writer whose Socratic works survive, also portrays Socrates at a symposium (and with love as the topic of conversation too). He was not as well off as the people who formed the nucleus of his circle, but his fame and influence among them was so great that he would certainly have been on their guest-lists. The setting is no artificial device of Plato's, and the attitudes Socrates' fellow-symposiasts display towards him—chiefly deep respect, tempered with banter—are just as natural and realistic.

The symposium was an institution of upper-class Athenian life. The literal translation of the word, 'drinks party', has misleading connotations for an English reader, so it is best simply to transliterate it. The consumption of alcohol was indeed the main purpose of the party, but the evening meal would have been eaten first. The guests would all be men; their host would provide them with chaplets and perfume, and they would recline in a half-lying position on couches. Their left arms rested on cushions and supported the upper half of their bodies, so that their right hands were free for eating and drinking from the table in front of them, and for whatever other activities might occur later on.

After dinner religious libations were poured and a hymn of praise to the gods was sung. A sip of neat wine consecrated the drink and initiated the actual symposium. The drink was wine diluted with water, and, unless or until things got out of hand, the proportion of water and the quantity of alcohol consumed would have been regulated by a president. During this phase of the party the host would probably have provided entertainment, if he could afford to, in the form of hired female pipe-players, and/or dancers, acrobats, and mimes. It was not at all uncommon for the pipe-players to double as sexual partners for any guests who felt so inclined: the pipe-players would be slaves, and that was one of the acknowledged uses to which Greek men could put female slaves. Otherwise, the guests would follow up the entertainment by amusing themselves with conversation, songs, riddles, and party-games. It was very much an all-male preserve, and it would be an unusual symposium which catered for the presence of respectable women.

At the party which forms the setting of our book, the symposiasts urbanely agree to dismiss the hired entertainment and amuse themselves by delivering speeches in praise of the god, Love personified. They speak 'from left to right', beginning with Phaedrus, who has the 'first' couch, and ending with Socrates who shares the 'end' couch with Agathon (175c, 177d). So the couches must have been arranged in a rough circle, horseshoe or oblong, though it is not clear by what criterion a couch was named 'first' or 'last': perhaps it was traditional for the host to defer to his guests by taking the couch furthest from the entrance to the kitchen, so that he would be served last.

The first couch is occupied by Phaedrus; there are then a number of other unnamed guests (180c), some of whom may or may not be sharing couches with Phaedrus and the next named guest, who is Pausanias (for biographical details of named guests, see the Index of Names). Then Aristophanes (whom we are surely to picture as alone on a couch: see the note on 193a), is followed by Eryximachus and Aristodemus, who share. Agathon and Socrates have the final couch. Since a common number of couches for a good-sized Athenian dining-room was seven (or nine), we may speculate that the unnamed guests fill two couches, and Agathon's dining-room is a seven-couch room. There is space around the outside of the couches, where slaves wait to serve the guests; and the arrangement also allows slaves to enter the circle to attend to the low tables by each couch. By the end of the dialogue, so many other people have joined the party that in all likelihood they were sprawled on the floor as well as sharing three to a couch. The reader should also imagine the room as well lit with many oil-lamps, and should remember that the walls would have been covered with colourful representations of great scenes from myth and legend, perhaps, and that their drinking-cups and other utensils would also have been decorated with figures.

Homoeroticism

So speeches on love are delivered by each of the guests in turn—and every single speech in some way or other has homoerotic love in the background or foreground. Here is another feature of Athenian life that needs some explanation, and some readers may well have to shed prejudices and preconceptions if they are to enjoy the dialogue properly.

In ancient Athens, homoeroticism was considered perfectly natural, especially in the leisured classes. I use the less familiar term 'homoeroticism' because not many Athenians were actually homosexual in the sense of being inclined to love *only* members of their own sex: Pausanias and Agathon in our dialogue, with their lifelong affair, were exceptions rather than the rule. More commonly, the same people were sexually inclined towards members of both sexes; and Athenian society did not regard the homoerotic element as perverted and the heteroerotic element as normal. Moreover, the boys who were the objects of male homoeroticism were not (at any rate in Plato's time) admired because they resembled girls: in other words, the Athenian phenomenon was homoeroticism, not repressed heteroeroticism.

There are undoubtedly social factors at work here. Any society which represses its women as much as ancient Athens did runs the risk of forcing its members to find other outlets for their sexuality. Respectable Athenian women would rarely even be seen on the street; their job was to keep house and bring up the children. This impedes the normal interplay between men and women which underpins a heterosexual society. This is why homoeroticism was more of an upper-class phenomenon: spacious residences allowed these men to segregate their women more thoroughly. Moreover, their marriages were rarely for love. And another social factor was the risk of unwanted births; men practised anal intercourse, and intercourse between the thighs, with women as well as with their boyfriends.

In a patriarchal society men tend to regard their partners as subordinate (and even to use sex as a means of asserting their dominance). This led to certain norms of behaviour in a homoerotic context. Typically, the objects of male homoerotic desires were young boys in their teens, between the ages of puberty and growth of a proper beard. A good-looking boy could expect to have a number of older *erastai* (lovers, or literally men feeling *erōs* for him). They would each pursue him, and try to persuade him to consummate a sexual affair, while he was expected to be coy and to resist their blandishments. The boy might, of course, eventually be won over by one of his lovers, but even then there was no equality of desire. He was expected to be merely passive, to let the man have his way, to 'gratify' the lover (as the Greeks tended rather delicately to put it): the lover would achieve the enjoyment at least of conquest and of sexual release, while the boy might at the most reciprocate with *philia* (loyal affection or friendship), which would be due for the lover's patronage (for future political advancement, perhaps), rather than for his sexual attentions. That is why only the older man is a 'lover', while the boy is merely an *erōmenos*—an object of the lover's *erōs*.

Socrates' Attitude Towards Homoeroticism

To say that homoeroticism was acceptable within Athenian society is not to say that any given member of the society accepted it. Socrates' is one of the few dissenting voices we hear (note that I am not here going to try to disentangle Socrates' from Plato's views).

The first point to notice is that a homoerotic element is very common in Plato's early dialogues (and in Xenophon's works too, although he tends to play it down). It is not just that the people Socrates is with are often portrayed as being in love with young boys (as at, say, *Lysis* 204b ff.); Socrates himself is portrayed as being attracted towards the charms of young men (most famously at *Charmides* 154b ff., especially 155d). His 'affair' with Alcibiades, which features so prominently in

Symposium, was apparently a point on which his friends used to tease him (*Protagoras* 309a). In short, he is commonly portrayed as being an *erastēs* of the young men in his circle.

Plato, then, certainly portrays Socrates as attracted towards young men and boys. This should not shock us by now, since we have seen that this was perfectly normal behaviour at the time in Athens. However, it also seems undeniable that Plato portrays him as a very odd kind of *erastēs*. The primary piece of evidence, for readers of *Symposium*, is the famous story Alcibiades tells at the end of the dialogue of Socrates' indifference to his charms and refusal to have sex with him. If this were a unique piece of evidence, we might think that it was specially composed for the purposes of this particular dialogue: Diotima has just argued that physical sex is not the be-all and end-all of *erōs*, and Alcibiades confirms that Socrates is someone who has taken that lesson to heart.

However, there is plenty of other evidence. Socrates' reported comments on homoerotic sex range from devaluing it in preference to love of the mind, to banning it altogether (Xenophon, *Symposium* 4. 26, 8. 12, 8. 32, *Memorabilia* 1. 2. 29, 1. 3. 8–13; Plato, *Republic* 403b, *Phaedrus* 250e–251a; see also Plato, *Laws* 636a–c, 836c–841e, though these sentiments are not put into Socrates' mouth). So if Socrates was portrayed as attracted to young men, he also seems to have exercised self-restraint, and to have disapproved of the sexual side of homoerotic love. Homoeroticism is not unnatural if one defines what is natural as what creatures do; but it is unnatural if one defines the natural purpose of sex as procreation. The emphasis placed on procreation in Socrates' speech in *Symposium* would lead one to think that he fell into the latter class.

It seems likely that Socrates exploited the homoerotic nature of the Athenian circle within which he moved for his own ends. If he played the lover and pursued young men, he was trying to make them consummate a lifelong affair with philosophy, not with himself; he turned the 'patronage' of the lover (as I called it a short while ago) to educational purposes. There is no doubt that, for all his physical ugliness (see the note on 215b), he could be immensely charismatic. This enabled him to effect a role-reversal. His disciples, though younger, become his 'lovers' (173b, 217c, 222b); though beauty and youth are commonly regarded as the natural objects of *erōs*, ugly old Socrates is loved by his young friends. In Athenian terms, this is an exquisite paradox. In Socrates' terms, the desire of a young man had to be aroused, even if the young man mistakenly took it at first to be physical, because that same desire could enable him to transcend the physical and pursue wisdom and knowledge (see 210a–212a).

In *Symposium* Diotima argues in the abstract for an equivalent role-reversal: the older man in a homoerotic relationship becomes a metaphorical woman in the sense that he gives birth to beautiful educational arguments for the sake of his young boyfriend (see the note on 206c). Alcibiades then enters and, in this as in so much else, confirms that Socrates lives up to Diotima's teaching. Socrates is not only Love in person, in the sense that the place occupied by Love in the others' speeches is occupied by Socrates in Alcibiades' speech; he is also Philosophy in person. The master–pupil relationship in philosophical training is erotic in that the master embodies the wisdom the pupil desires; but it is a mistake to downgrade this eroticism and have sex with your teacher (a number of notorious gurus in the West in recent years would have done well to note this). In all this it is never far from the surface that the Greek word *philosophia* means 'love of wisdom'. For those Greeks who took it seriously, philosophy was more than higher education: it was a way of life and a means of salvation. It was therefore to be pursued passionately, with lifelong devotion; even in other dialogues we commonly find Plato resorting to sexual imagery to describe the philosopher's attitude towards philosophy.

The Artistry of the Dialogue

The kind of interplay between one part of *Symposium* and another to which I have just drawn attention is a very important feature of the dialogue. The bulk of the dialogue consists of a series of seven speeches, and there are constant echoes between them, some of which are acknowledged, while others are left for the reader to pick up by himself. Here we are glimpsing an aspect of the artistry of the dialogue, for which it is justly famous.

It is notoriously difficult to discuss the artistry of a piece of work: one rapidly enters upon areas of subjectivity. Still, apart from the feature which I have just mentioned, I would add two or three more with some degree of confidence.

There is the fact that each of the speeches is quite different from any other. Plato writes in seven different styles in the course of the dialogue, and anyone who has tried his hand at writing knows how difficult it is to add even one new style to the one which comes naturally to him. Some of the differences between the speeches are hard or impossible to capture in English, since they depend on various devices of ancient Greek rhetoric: Phaedrus' speech is reminiscent of the orator Lysias, for example, while Agathon's is of Gorgias; Pausanias uses more isocolon (phrases of equal or roughly equal length) than the others; and so on. The artistry here lies not just in Plato's imitation of different styles, but in the characterization of each of the speakers by that means. However, although it is clear that each of the speakers is characterized differently, it is very hard to be more precise. Is Phaedrus shallow or economical? Is Eryximachus pompous or profound? Is Aristophanes sincere or satirical? We do not quite know how to read any of the speeches.

On this I should say that it is extremely likely that our appreciation of the work would be increased if we knew more about the lives of more of the characters (who are all real people, apart from Socrates' mentor Diotima). If we knew, for instance, that the historical Eryximachus was famous for lecturing people rather than talking to them as equals, then we would know with more certainty how to take his speech. We do know quite a lot about the historical Alcibiades, and the dialogue abounds in echoes from his life. Here is what Martha Nussbaum says about these echoes from Alcibiades' life (*The Fragility of Goodness*, 166):

A man who died shot by an arrow will speak of the words of love as arrows or bolts wounding the soul (219b). A man who influentially denounced the flute as an instrument unworthy of a free man's dignity will describe himself as a slave to the enchanting flute-playing of a certain satyr (215b–d, 216c, 219c). A man who will deface holy statues compares the soul of Socrates to a set of god-statues and speaks of the injustice of rubbing out, or defacing, Socratic virtues (213e, 215b, 216d, 217e, 222a). A man who will profane the mysteries puts on trial the initiate of the mystery-religion of *erōs*.

I would add that the profanation or performance of the Eleusinian Mysteries by Alcibiades was widely rumoured at the time to have occurred during a symposium.

Perhaps the most important aspect of the artistry of *Symposium* is the interplay between words and action. We are nowhere told in express words that we are to think of Socrates as Love and Philosophy embodied, or of Alcibiades as Dionysus or Beauty incarnate, but it is clear that we are meant to do so. Nor is this mere embellishment: the tension between calmness and frenzy is a vital theme of the dialogue. To a Greek, *erōs* meant primarily irrational desire, the kind of desire which could possess you and overwhelm you: that is why Plato firmly castigates it as a force for evil in *Republic* 571a–576b (see also *Phaedo* 83b–d). In Diotima's speech, this aspect of *erōs* becomes just one manifestation of a force that motivates us whatever we do, so that even the rational, calm desires of the philosopher are driven by the same force (see also the note on 220a). Diotima's vision of these 'higher mysteries' of Love contrasts with the underlying assumption of the earlier speakers that Love is a god and therefore irresistible. Alcibiades' frenzied speech in its turn contrasts with Diotima's crystalline calmness: he perhaps embodies philosophic love gone wrong, in that he swings in and out of Socrates' influence. Recognizing the importance of the theme to Plato (and the contrast between reason and emotion recurs often in his dialogues), one can only stand in awe of his confidence and daring in leaving it implicit and unstated, more or less up to the reader's unconscious grasp.

Others will find other aspects of the dialogue to admire in this context. I cannot leave the matter without trying to explain one of the most noticeable peculiarities of the dialogue, which is how many-layered Plato makes the narrative. Apollodorus (perhaps in 404 BC) is repeating to a group of unnamed friends a report he gave to Glaucon (a couple of days earlier) of Aristodemus' report (given when?) of the speeches which took place at a symposium in 416 BC. Although it was a standard feature of both Plato's and Xenophon's Socratic writings to pretend that they were reliable accounts of conversations of Socrates, Plato makes us doubt the accuracy of this account, by questioning the reliability of the reporters' memories (178a, 180c). Why does he distance us, his readers, so carefully from the events? I can only think that by drawing so much attention to how far we are from the symposium, he is actually inviting us to think what it would be like to have been there. He is aware that the blazing intensity of such occasions can only be faintly reproduced in writing. He is saying, 'You had to be there, to experience it. The most I can do is capture something of the atmosphere.' I doubt that many readers of *Symposium* would think that he had failed in this regard. There is nothing leaden about the light of the dialogue: Plato has captured a unique moment of cultural history under a high-powered beam, and one's recall of the symposium is always colourful, never in mere black and white.

The First Five Speeches

Detailed commentary on these speeches, as on other aspects of the dialogue, has been restricted to the notes. Here we have to consider their role within the dialogue as a whole.

First, however, it is worth noting that many of the general features of all the speeches are due simply to the fact that the speakers have undertaken to deliver an encomium of a god. The encomium was a particular type of speech, which had its own rules and features. Here is what the anonymous *Rhetorica ad Alexandrum*, which was written around 300 BC, has to say about the matter in section 35 (drawing on E. S. Forster's translation (*The Works of Aristotle Translated into English*, xi, London: Oxford University Press, 1924)):

After the proem, we must distinguish those good qualities of our subject which are outside the sphere of virtue and those which fall within it, as follows: those which fall outside the sphere of virtue we shall divide into good birth, physical strength, personal beauty and wealth, while we shall divide virtue into wisdom, justice, courage and noteworthy habits of life. The qualities which pertain to virtue are proper subjects of eulogy; those which fall outside virtue must be disguised ... We shall give the genealogy of the subject of our speech the first place after the proem ... If there is nothing distinguished in the ancestry of the subject of your eulogy, you must insist on his personal nobility and suggest that all those who have a natural predisposition for virtue are 'well born' ... You must next describe his habits and way of life ... You must also compare the notable achievements of other young men and show that his actions far surpass theirs, relating the least important of their deeds and the most important achievements of the subject of your eulogy.

And so on: the whole of the subject's life is dealt with under the headings of the cardinal virtues of moderation, courage, justice, and wisdom. In the first place, this excerpt shows the degree to which the speakers in *Symposium* (especially Phaedrus, Agathon, and, in odder ways, Diotima and Alcibiades) conform to the expected lineaments of an encomium; secondly, it shows the justice of Socrates' complaint about the previous speakers' dishonesty (198d ff.).

It is common, in considering the purpose of the first five speeches, to compare them to the speech of Socrates-Diotima. In what respects does Socrates disagree with them? In what respects does he develop points they made? Can they even be seen as forming a gradual progression, working towards the theory developed in Socrates' speech? How do they measure up to Socrates' moral standards?

The main difficulty with these kinds of questions is that there are as many points of convergence between Socrates' speech and the others as there are points of divergence. For instance, Pausanias claims that there are two kinds of love, good and bad; Socrates disagrees and prefers the view that there is only one love, which can be put to different uses. Nevertheless, Socrates agrees with Pausanias about the educational value of a proper homoerotic relationship. Or again, disagreement between Socrates and Aristophanes is expressly signalled at 205e, but there is an important resemblance between the two speeches in that they both distinguish between the conscious and unconscious objects of love. Or again (and finally, because the list could be expanded a lot), Socrates disagrees with Agathon as to the precise relationship between love and beauty, but agrees with him that it is crucial to take beauty into consideration when thinking about love.

In short, there are all kinds of interactions between all the speeches; there are interactions within the first five as well as between them and Socrates-Diotima. The contrast between Socrates as philosopher and Agathon as artist, for instance, is no more or less important and interesting than that between Agathon as artist and Eryximachus as craftsman. It is particularly hard to sustain the thesis that the first five speeches form some kind of progression: Aristophanes is certainly more profound than Agathon, and yet precedes him; there is a greater degree of morality (at least, ostensible morality) in Pausanias' speech than in any of the others, yet his speech comes only second; the broadness of Eryximachus' view of love fits well with Socrates' theories, yet Eryximachus' speech is clearly no kind of culmination. It seems best, then, to take each of the first five speeches at face value and to think of what it has to offer in itself, rather than to compare it to what Socrates says.

From Phaedrus' plain, and at times slightly awkward speech, we learn that love has been a force to be reckoned with since the beginning of time. Already in this first speech, love is shown to be a potent force for moral behaviour. Pausanias' chief function is to draw attention to the moral ambivalence of love and to the educational potential of a love-affair. Eryximachus (perhaps drawing on the work of the philosopher Empedocles) adds that love's power pervades everything. It is true that he tends to force phenomena to fit into his scheme (but so did all of the early scientists, in some way or other), but it is more important to notice that the sexual aspect of *erōs* becomes in his speech little more than a metaphor, once the reference of *erōs* has expanded beyond the boundaries of human relations.

Aristophanes' speech is bound to strike us as exceptional, for its Rabelaisian whimsy, its pathos, and its psychological insight. There is no telling how it would have struck an ancient reader, and, as I have already remarked, we cannot even be sure whether or not it is supposed to bring a smile to our lips. It certainly will if it is read with that assumption. Is it a satire on romantic love, or is it a sad commentary on the elusiveness of true happiness (which becomes dependent on the hazard of meeting one's true partner) and on the unsatisfactoriness of sex as a poor second best to the total unification we are really after? The distinction between our ostensible and underlying motivations seems very modern to us today, and the speech as a whole was appreciated by Freud. Halperin (1985, p. 169) is right to talk of 'Plato's unprecedented and shattering discovery that the genuine object of *erōs*—whatever it is—does not belong to the same order of reality as the objects intended by the human appetites'. However, it is easy to get carried away by the story Aristophanes tells, and to fail to consider whether or not we really want to agree with some of the other propositions Plato puts into his mouth—that our sexual preferences are innate rather than conditioned by society, and that we each have a perfect mate somewhere. Such reflections aside, there is no doubt that the point of the speech is to tell the story of love from the inside, to sketch what it actually feels like, in order to counterbalance the impersonality of some of the previous speeches. Love may be a cosmic universal force, but in human beings it is a longing for lost happiness. Diotima would agree that love can fulfil one's highest aspirations, but would disagree with quite how Aristophanes sees those aspirations being fulfilled, and she would also put more control over our happiness into our own hands rather than those of an external soul-mate.

Finally, Agathon's speech is little more than a *tour de force*, as Agathon himself is made to acknowledge at 197e (see the note on 197c). Nevertheless, as he also claims, some valuable points are made. The most important point, which becomes crucial in Diotima's speech, is that it is impossible to talk about love without talking about beauty. He also continues the approach which Aristophanes began, of thinking about what it is like for a human being to be in love: Agathon tends to attribute to Love all the nice things we feel and notice around us when we are in love. The lasting impression his speech gives is that Love is pretty, and to Greek ears his speech too would have been pretty. Underneath the pretty exterior lies a conventional encomium and a conventional view of Love, which reflects the god's portraits we can find in paintings and in literature. It is therefore a perfect speech for Agathon the artist. It is Agathon's night: the party is in celebration of his victory. If we are also left with the impression from his speech that Love is somewhat self-satisfied, then that too may well have been intended by Plato.

Socrates' Speech

After ironically criticizing the previous speakers' dishonesty, Socrates begins his substantial part in the dialogue by cross-questioning Agathon in a manner reminiscent of many of Plato's early dialogues. Basing himself firmly on Agathon's own beliefs, Socrates 'proves' that if Love's object is beauty, then Love is not beautiful. This seems a rather trivial point to us, since we find it hard to conceive of Love as a god, rather than a relation. An ancient Greek, however, would have been reluctant to concede that the god Love was not attractive, and so, if he was persuaded by Socrates' rather bad argument, he would have had to concede that love's object is not beauty. This is the point Socrates wants to establish. He does believe that love and beauty are intrinsically connected, but not quite in the straightforward way Agathon had claimed.

In order to clarify the truth of the matter, he introduces the Mantinean priestess Diotima who, he claims, taught him all he knows about love—the delicious ambiguity is perfectly deliberate. Some possible reasons for the device of introducing a third party are mentioned in the Index of Names, under 'Diotima'; and some of the particular complexities of the position Diotima develops are discussed in the notes on her speech.

Socrates' argument with Agathon merges with Diotima's argument with Socrates (201e), so we can safely consider them together. The following points are made (I have not necessarily quite followed the order of the actual argument as it occurs in the text):

1. Love is a kind of desire, which is to say that it is always love *of* something (199e).

2. This something which love desires is something which it lacks (200a).

3. This something which love desires is something which it wants to have, or (if it already has it) to continue to have (200a–e).

4. It follows that if Love loves beauty, then Love lacks beauty, and is not beautiful, and wants to possess beauty (201a–b).

5. But in fact what people always love is goodness, not beauty exactly—which is to say they long to be happy and fulfilled. This is the universal human condition (204e–205a).

6. This love which has to do with beauty is actually, then, only a fraction of what love is. Love in general is for goodness; 'love' as the word is commonly used has something to do with beauty, but must actually be for goodness and happiness (205b–e).

7. No one wants goodness temporarily; they want it for ever (206a).

8. To want something for ever is in a covert form to want immortality (207a).

9. Immortality is more or less impossible for a person *qua* the particular person he is. We all change from moment to moment; we merely give the impression of identity by replacing one generation of traits, features, and so on, with another generation, which resembles the preceding one (207d–208b).

10. Relative immortality can only be achieved through procreation of some kind—for instance, by perpetuating oneself through one's children or through producing long-lasting works of art (208c–209e).

11. Procreation is impossible for a person in a medium which he finds repellent (206c–d).

12. Procreation can only take place in a beautiful medium; the connection between love and beauty is therefore that the desire for immortality—for goodness for ever—requires a beautiful medium (206e–207a).

This is a truly extraordinary argument. Immortality slips in through a side door, as does love of goodness; steps 4 and 8 are blatantly fallacious. Yet these sophisms blend with insights of great profundity. It is clear that the insights are what are important to Plato, and that the logic of how he persuades his readers of these insights is secondary. I shall therefore here concentrate on the insights rather than picking on the fallacies, which are best left to the appropriate notes.

The insights which control the argument are chiefly these:

A. The deficiency model (as it has been called) of love; the assimilation of love and desire; love as an in-between state.

B. The fact that the desire for happiness, which is to say the desire for goodness, is what motivates and underlies all our actions, big and small, all the time. What we usually call 'love' is just a particular manifestation of this universal motivating force.

C. We would like to be immortal.

D. We are inherently creative.

These last two insights actually converge in Plato's mind. He finds it relatively simple to demonstrate human creativity by appealing to a range of phenomena, from the instinctive demand (which is common to all species) that we should bear and raise offspring, to the particular creativity of artists and legislators. But in creating such offspring we are simultaneously striving to perpetuate ourselves. We (in some sense of 'we') are driven to outlive ourselves. Even apart from the fact that as a species we are constantly exploring and trying to do better, at a lower level consider, for instance, the drive for wealth: somewhere in our minds we know that this is futile, because we cannot take it with us when we die. We justify it by saying that we will leave it to our children.

The universality of the desire for happiness is as absolute an axiom for Plato as it was for all Greeks. The word for which the best available translation is 'happiness' (*eudaimonia*) was always used to refer to the ideal state, however you conceived it to be. If you think a life of unalloyed sensual pleasure is what constitutes happiness, then that is what you will strive for. In *Symposium* Plato is taking for granted more extended arguments such as that of *Euthydemus* 278e ff., in which he analyses the desire for happiness into a desire for the possession of good things (again, however those are conceived) and for the ability to put them to proper, profitable use. There are still philosophical controversies in this area, but at an overall level, it is hard to argue against this axiom of Greek thinking.

The same cannot be said for Plato's final insight, the assimilation of love and desire. Is love really as self-centred and as need-fulfilling as desire? Plato provides little back-up for this assertion. Although he goes on at some length about it, he supports it only by means of two tales which it is easier for us nowadays to interpret metaphorically than literally. The first claims that Love is not a god, but a spirit (*daimōn*), and the second is the allegory of Love's birth as the child of Plenty and Poverty. The point of both stories is simply to reinforce the notion that Love is imperfect and is in need; in other words, they are not meant to be reasoned arguments in support of the deficiency model, and so they take us no further towards uncovering Plato's underlying thinking. We will have to return to the deficiency model a little later, after surveying the rest of Diotima's speech.

The Ascent

Diotima goes on to give a dazzling picture of the potential value of love in our lives. Her premise is that we can transfer the affection which carries our love from a given object on to another, more capacious object, and so ascend through various levels to a vision of absolute beauty. The almost religious fervour of her words is in keeping with her description of her speech as an initiation into a mystery cult. The cross-examination of Socrates serves as the initiatory purification, then the neophyte is instructed in the matters pertaining to the cult, and finally the candidate is afforded a vision of the heart of the mystery. 'This side of Diotima's philosophizing,' Bury points out (p. xlix), 'which brings into full light what we may call as we please either the erotic aspect of religion or the religious aspect of Eros, might be illustrated abundantly both from the writers of romantic love-poetry and from the religious mystics.' It is not surprising that this aspect of Diotima's speech has become one of the favourite sources for religious and mystical writers in the West. Plotinus describes the ascent to the One in terms which consciously echo *Symposium* (*Enneads* 1. 6. 8–9). Similar echoes occur in Origen's description of the soul's renunciation of the things of the world and advancing to perfect knowledge and the contemplation of a pure realm of causes (*De Principiis* II. xi. 7). Diotima gave Augustine the words to express his mystical vision at Ostia (*Confessions* 9. 10). In short, it sometimes seems as though it has become virtually impossible for the experience of spiritual ascent not to be clothed in the terminology of Diotima's speech.

There are, however, a number of obscurities in Diotima's description of the ascent (210a–212a), and a great deal of valuable scholarly work has gone into analysing the passage. I cannot here summarize the debate, so my account will have to be dogmatic; it owes the most to A. W. Price's account in *Love and Friendship in Plato and Aristotle*. There are essentially four levels: physical beauty, mental beauty, the beauty of 'intellectual endeavours', and finally absolute beauty. At each stage, an act of intellectual generalization takes place. At the physical level, you appreciate rationally that the same features you find beautiful in your beloved can be found in countless other people. (Note that this does not license promiscuity: the appreciation of physical beauty is not the same as the lustful pursuit of it!) Mental beauty is manifested in 'activities and institutions', and at this level too you appreciate that the particular activities and institutions you start by finding beautiful are really no more or less beautiful than the activities and institutions which other people or countries have produced. Similarly (although the text is considerably less clear at this point) we are to suppose that we move within the level of knowledge from being attracted to one particular branch of knowledge to becoming philosophers—that is, to loving knowledge in general.

The other role that reason plays at each level is to make us think less of the kind of beauty we are beginning to rise above. There is no reason to think that we entirely cease to be attracted towards the lesser beauty of the things we have somehow left behind; but it is certainly clear from Diotima's words that we think considerably less of them. Their beauty pales into insignificance.

However, all this takes place *within* each level. What enables us to move between levels, from one level to the next? Diotima chooses to leave the matter utterly unclear. It may be important to remember that one is supposed to have a guide during this journey. Perhaps it is the guide's role to shift us from one level to the next, and perhaps the guide does this by rational argument—by arguing us out of our fixed and cherished notions, as Socrates does. This would be perfectly Platonic, but I cannot help thinking that it is not enough. One of the most remarkable and incomprehensible features of the passage is the unstated assumption that each level of the ascent becomes one's permanent state of being; there is no talk of backsliding. Could even Socratic argument persuade me to change my life so thoroughly? Perhaps, if it is repeated often enough, and Plato certainly represents Socrates as stressing the value of repeating arguments to oneself, until conviction changes to knowledge.

I am also sure, however, that for all the high-flown language, the basis of the ascent is an experience familiar to all of us—the expansive nature of love. If I am in love, many things about the world, not just the immediate object of my love, seem lovable. To say 'I love X' is somehow really to say 'X inspires love in me', and that love then attaches itself to objects other than X as well. The expansiveness of love is a natural means of ascent between levels.

Diotima leaves us to guess, but it seems plausible to suggest that it is the *combination* of reason and emotion that not only enables the ascent between stages to take place, but also makes it possible for it to gain some degree of permanence once it has taken place. If reason leads, emotion follows; if emotion leads, reason follows. As Plato argues in *Republic* (e.g. 440c), reason stabilizes the fickleness of emotion, and emotion gives meaning to the dictates of reason. For anyone familiar with Plato's *Republic*, there are important echoes here. The ascent may be seen as the release of reason from being bound up in the lower parts of the mind until it is free to do its proper job and take control of a person's life. What Plato adds in *Symposium* to the doctrine of *Republic* is the role of love in this. Love is what gives us the potential (which we may seize or waste as we choose) to pull ourselves out of the mire of the bestial side of our nature. It is human nature to be in love, to have aspirations beyond the human condition, to be *daimōn*-like.

The penultimate phase of the ascent is the study of philosophy. This will eventually enable one to appreciate that all beautiful objects share some common characteristic. This characteristic, which is what it is to be beautiful, cannot be any particular manifestation of beauty, because that would prevent other manifestations from being beautiful. Nor is it relatively beautiful in any other respect. It is absolutely and perfectly beautiful. Once this has been appreciated, love can find only this object perfectly fulfilling of its desires.

The temptation to talk about the ascent in terms of sublimation of erotic impulses has proved too strong for some post-Freudian commentators, but it is entirely inappropriate. Diotima is not talking about the unconscious repression of instinctive energy, but the conscious transcendence of it. Whatever precisely Freud meant by the term 'sublimation' (he changed his mind a number of times about it), it seems to involve a blockage of the erotic impulse; in Diotima's speech, on the other hand, *erōs* is never blocked, even though it may be transferred on to different objects. Even here there is a difference between Plato and Freud: the new objects of *erōs* in Freudian sublimation are less satisfactory than the objects the person really desires; for Diotima, however, the further up the ladder of love one ascends, the more fulfilling the objects are. Finally, although it is clear that the passion of *erōs* is preserved throughout the ascent, it is not clear that the sexual element is, except as a metaphor (as in Eryximachus' speech); for Freud, however, sublimated desires remained essentially sexual.

In Aristophanes' speech, sexual desire is a sort of cosmic error, a result of our primordial splitting, something which should never have happened had the human race not misbehaved. For Plato too sex is a mistake: 'Any lover who sets about to translate his supposed physical attraction into sexual activity has in effect substituted the body of his beloved for the beauty in it that attracts him and has thus doomed himself to an enslaving (*Symposium* 210d3; cf. 219e3–4) and frustrating obsession' (Halperin, 1985, p. 182). Sex is one of those things which act as nails, joining the soul to the body (*Phaedo* 83d), when it should be free. One should rechannel sexual *erōs* into more worthwhile goals (*Laws* 839e–841c; on the image of 'rechannelling', see *Republic* 485d–e). However, some sexual activity is important for health (*Timaeus* 91b–c) and to prevent the mind being distracted by insistent physical desires (*Symposium* 191c), so that it can get on with its proper activity, which for Plato means striving for the kind of goal Diotima describes.

There is no doubt that the absolute beauty of which Plato speaks here is one of those metaphysical entities which occasionally put in an appearance in his dialogues, and which are commonly (but misleadingly) referred to as Forms. The reader may be referred to *Phaedo* and the central sections of *Republic* for Plato's main discussions on this topic. Briefly, Plato believed that the beauty of beautiful things could only be explained by their participation in or reflection of an abstract entity, beauty itself. There must be some single, unchanging entity to be the object of reference of our statements and thoughts about the particular beauty of beautiful things; otherwise, we are condemned to relativity and solipsism, and there could be no certainty or knowledge about things such as beauty. For in the world around us there is no such thing as perfect beauty: anything we describe as beautiful is, from another point of view or to a different perceiver, not beautiful. From where else, then, except from a subliminal knowledge of the Form, absolute beauty, could we have acquired a standard by which to judge things as beautiful?

However, most of what Plato has to say in *Symposium* is comprehensible without understanding anything about his metaphysical theories: we need only think of the Form, beauty, as some kind of absolute. *Symposium* adds little to the metaphysics, ontology, and epistemology of his other middle-period dialogues, except a fuller description of the ways in which the

Forms are non-relative; but it adds superbly to the psychology. Even the status of absolute beauty is unclear: is it merely one Form, on a par with the rest, or is it somehow supreme, like goodness in *Republic*? Or is it even in some sense the beauty of the world of Forms in general?

Finally, it is easy to lose sight in this part of Diotima's speech of the fact that love's desire is for immortality through procreation. What do we procreate at each stage of the ascent? Again, Plato chooses not to make things perfectly clear, but there must be room for all the creations he has previously mentioned (except for actual children, since homoerotic love is the background here—211b); these offspring of 'mental' pregnancy are above all virtuous deeds, educational discussions, works of art, and legislation (208c–209e). Ultimately, the intercourse between a philosopher and perfect beauty results in the birth of true virtue (212a) and enables him to attain immortality. This is probably a reference to Plato's teaching that truly virtuous people do not have to be reincarnated any more, but live in a disembodied form in everlasting bliss. Did George Herbert have this aspect of Diotima's teaching in mind when composing the last verse of his poem 'Virtue'?

> Only a sweet and virtuous soul,
> Like season'd timber, never gives;
> But though the whole world turn to coal,
> Then chiefly lives.

Diotima's reminder, at the very end of her speech, of the relation between love and immortality invites us to think that, whatever the offspring at each level are, the offspring of higher levels are longer-lasting than those of lower levels. So too with the objects found beautiful at each stage. Physical beauty fades fast, as the Greeks were for ever stressing; human activities and institutions change gradually over time, or vary from culture to culture; even what we call knowledge may be superseded in time; the only certainty, in Plato's terms, is beauty itself. Moreover, we are also supposed to think of an ever-widening circle, starting from my personal perception of beauty in another person, and expanding out through objects which greater and greater numbers of people are bound to find beautiful; again, the goal is absolute beauty, which cannot by definition be found by anyone to lack beauty in any respect. Diotima's extraordinary vision is powerful, and moves us, precisely because of our innate need for perfect love. We know that individuals and objects will let us down; she offers us something which will not and cannot disappoint us.

Love in Plato

It is still possible to read in the literature the idea that for Plato beauty is the object of love. But this is wrong: this is Agathon's idea, and it is explicitly denied by Diotima (although it is true that she sometimes uses a kind of shorthand which slightly confuses the issue). It is not beauty which is the object, but happiness, which in turn is defined as the permanent possession of goodness. Beauty is our means to that goal, in the sense that in its various manifestations it is our partner—the medium or receptacle in which we can give birth to children who will guarantee, or who we think will guarantee, our happiness. We may be attracted towards beauty, but our real goal is happiness.

In outlining the 'higher mysteries of love', Diotima stops talking about love as a relationship between people and takes off into the stratosphere where love becomes philosophy and the means of man's fulfilment as a human being. But this is a change of perspective, not a change of direction. She has already insisted that love between people is merely one manifestation of a pervasive motivating force in us; philosophy is simply the highest manifestation of the same energy which at its lowest manifests as physical lust. We all want happiness and everything we do is supposed to bring us closer to that goal; falling in love with another person is just one way in which we seek to achieve that. If love in general aims for goodness and immortality, the manifestation of that in the particular instance of inter-personal relationships is the aim of procreation in a beautiful medium (206b ff.).

This analysis of inter-personal love has been criticized as egoistic and cold. Plato seems to be saying that I should love other people not for themselves, but only for their qualities—

above all, the beauty they happen to possess—and only as a means towards the end of my own happiness.

There are in fact huge conceptual difficulties in the ideal of loving another person 'for himself' or 'for herself' as opposed to his or her qualities (what is a quality-less person? is it lovable?), but this is not the place to go into them. It is sufficient for our purposes to reply that the idea that we are driven by our desire for happiness is not intended by Plato to be a description of our feelings in a relationship. It is a piece of depth psychology. It is an analysis of what *underlies* the relationship; Diotima agrees with Aristophanes that there is more to love than meets the eye. The relationship itself, the affection I feel for the other person, may conform to whatever ideal of inter-personal love you care to hold, but that does not say anything either for or against Plato's analysis of underlying motivation. So if Plato spends little time on inter-personal love in *Symposium*, that does not mean that he devalues it, but only that it is not his purpose to analyse it in itself. His purpose is to analyse what underlies it, and what also underlies everything we do.

This bears crucially on Plato's deficiency model—his assimilation of love and desire. This assimilation is not as crude as a careless reading of the dialogue might suggest. He does not say that if I love something, I desire to possess it for ever. He says that whatever you love, your *underlying* motivation is the permanent possession of goodness. In other words, the reason we love (desire perfection) is precisely because it is the human condition not to be perfect instances of anything. Love involves deficiencies and awareness of deficiencies. One has to be dissatisfied to be motivated at all; hence *all* desire is desire for goodness, for remedying an unsatisfactory state of affairs. By a clever piece of artistry, Diotima's concluding vision implicitly corroborates our awareness of our deficiencies: she holds out the promise of perfect love and perfect fulfilment, and if we find the promise at all attractive, that can only remind us of our own imperfect state.

So it is not enough just to accuse Plato's conception of inter-personal love of being self-centred. One would have to prove that love is not a kind of motivation, and that all motivation is not describable as a desire to remedy some defect. It is true that in the course of the argument with Agathon (199b–201c) Socrates argues for the position that to love something is to desire to possess it. In fact, this is not a misconceived notion. The language of 'possession' here springs from the fact that the discussion is couched in terms of the possession of properties, such as strength and health. There is nothing to prevent us interpreting 'desire for possession' as, in inter-personal relationships, 'desire to be with'. By the same token, we can interpret 'desire to possess something lacked' as 'desire to be with something or someone other than oneself'. It is hard to deny that these are essential elements of inter-personal love.

In any case, the argument with Agathon is promissory. It is best read as an incomplete statement of the position Diotima develops more fully a little later. And that, as we have seen, is not intended to be a description of the surface of love, but an analysis of its depths.

Having understood this, it is not clear that Plato's conception is altogether egoistic. To say that love is the desire for happiness begs an important question—in what does my happiness lie? There is plenty of evidence, particularly from *Republic*, that Plato is what we might call a moral egoist. My pursuit of happiness can paradoxically only be fulfilled if I promote the happiness of others. The evidence for this within *Symposium* lies in the fact that love is essentially, according to Diotima, the desire for procreation. Ultimately, the philosopher's intercourse with perfect beauty generates a character which manifests in genuinely virtuous behaviour towards other people. In *Republic* Plato's ultimate position is that the philosopher's purpose is to perpetuate goodness in the world. There is nothing in *Symposium* which is incompatible with this aim. Love in Diotima's speech is as much a desire to give as a desire to get. At each stage of the ascent, one attains the object of one's desire, and that leads one to procreate offspring which help to perpetuate an ever-widening moral environment.

The only word available in Greek for Plato to try to communicate this idea of an energy-source which empowers and motivates us in everything we do, however crude or sublime, was *erōs*. The only word available in English is 'love'.

Both words are familiarly associated with ideas that lie just below the surface of *Symposium*. Love is unsettling, and it is certain that the ascent of Diotima's ladder would turn one's life completely upside down. Love is a form of madness, then—though Plato will add in *Phaedrus* that madness may be either destructive or divine. (There are faint echoes here of Pausanias' distinction between Common and Celestial Love, and it may be worth noting that when this distinction crops up in Xenophon's *Symposium*, it is Socrates himself who makes it.) Love is a powerful, primeval force, as Phaedrus had said; love may be good or bad, as Pausanias had said; love is all-pervasive, as Eryximachus had said; love can be fulfilling or unfulfilling, as Aristophanes had said. Only Agathon's speech seems to contain nothing with which Socrates can quite agree, and this of course is why it is the last speech of the initial sequence, and why Agathon is the one who is subjected to some Socratic cross-questioning.

Alcibiades' Speech

But what of Alcibiades? Plato chooses not to leave us with the climax of Diotima, but to bring us down to earth. No reader of the dialogue will think that Alcibiades' speech is in some sense an appendix, however, awkwardly tacked on to the end. Somehow it seems to round the book off. Some of the resonances between Alcibiades' speech and earlier phases of the dialogue are fairly obvious, but some are elusive. The answers to two questions should pull most of the threads together. What do we see of Socrates in Alcibiades' speech? And what are we supposed to think of Alcibiades' character?

It is obvious that Socrates in Alcibiades' speech is meant to embody Diotima's teaching. We are given a vivid portrait of a philosopher who has rechannelled his *erōs* away from physical lust. Alcibiades was the best catch in Athens at the time. From among all those who were in love with him, he chose to offer himself to Socrates, and yet Socrates refused to have sex with him. The substitution of Socrates for Love is obvious (p. xviii), and we have just heard in Diotima's speech how Love is a philosopher (204a–b) and how in the higher mysteries of love the lover becomes a philosopher (210d); again, Socrates is clearly the archetypal philosopher. Alcibiades presents us with the paradox of Socrates: he is ugly but attractive, sexy but asexual, a restrained Satyr, his brutal saviour. Socrates, in other words, is in the kind of in-between state we would expect from him as Love incarnate, since Love is a *daimōn* and all *daimones* are in that state (202d–203a).

However, at least some of this is what *we* may see about Socrates in Alcibiades' speech, because we have been privy to Diotima's speech. Alcibiades only enters the picture after Socrates has finished recounting Diotima's speech: he has not heard any of it. *His* reason for speaking in praise of Socrates is that he is afraid of Socrates' jealousy (214c–d). By the time his speech is over, however, we are bound to think that in charging Socrates with jealousy he is indulging in wishful thinking: Socrates can no more be subject to base emotions such as jealousy than he can be overcome by drink.

Plato is well aware that anyone who tries to live by Diotima's ideals may seem cold and heartless where personal relationships are concerned. Socrates' purpose in life was not restricted to Alcibiades. He could not devote himself to a single young man in the way that lovers were expected to (183a); there were a number of young men in his circle (222b). In fact, his mission concerned the whole of Athens: at *Apology* 30d ff. Plato has Socrates describe himself as a gift of God to the city, a gadfly sent to disturb it from its dozy state. Yet as we read Plato's and Xenophon's Socratic works, we gain the impression that however apparently harsh he is with the people who are at the receiving end of his sometimes merciless arguments, he cares deeply for them. And as we hear the story of his spurning Alcibiades' approaches, we are bound (in the light of Diotima's teaching) to think that he cares deeply enough for Alcibiades to try to rechannel his *erōs* away from bodily lust and towards philosophy.

The interplay between Alcibiades' unwitting comments and how we read Alcibiades' speech in the light of having heard Diotima reaches an exquisite peak in 219d ff., where Alcibiades assigns to Socrates all the traditional virtues. From his point of view, all he is doing is delivering (or possibly parodying) a standard encomium, which required one to assign the virtues to one's subject (see pp. xxi–xxii). We, however, are bound to remember that, according to Diotima, virtue—stable virtue of the kind Socrates displays in Alcibiades' account—is the product of the philosopher's intercourse with absolute beauty. And then the additional irony is that the soldiers who witnessed Socrates' endurance during a military campaign, and who represent the citizens who will be called on to judge Socrates in his trial, think that his display of virtue is somehow intended to mock them (220b). Socrates/Love/Philosophy is too sublime for Alcibiades and others to understand; that takes total, unremitting devotion.

The fact that Alcibiades has not heard Diotima's speech is supposed to make us think that in certain important respects he does not understand Socrates at all, despite his boast that Socrates revealed himself to him and him alone (216e–217a). For Alcibiades, Socrates is bound to remain a puzzle: he can recognize his extraordinary uniqueness (221d), but cannot understand it. Although the aptness of the Silenus image shows that he does have certain insights into Socrates' character and the nature of his argumentation, and although he is deeply moved by Socrates, he fails to be fully converted to a philosophic way of life, and is still capable of succumbing to worldly temptations (216b).

The fact that Socrates is a paradox to Alcibiades in turn creates a tension in how we assess Alcibiades himself. One part of us sympathizes with him and his sorry tale of unrequited love; but then we remember that Socrates is meant to be our ideal and we disapprove of Alcibiades for being so stubbornly erotic (in some lower sense of the term). This causes us to look more carefully at what he is saying, and then we find there hints of instability. He confesses his love for Socrates and yet wants him dead (216c); he is fascinated by him and yet can be tempted away from him (216b); he is obsessive rather than broad-minded (215d).

In short, Alcibiades is a thorough mixture of good and bad. We feel that for all the naïve candour and confessional tone of his speech, he is ultimately too weak and wayward to be saved by Socrates or anyone else. And, of course, Plato's original audience would remember his subsequent history, which confirms this assessment (see the Index of Names). If Socrates is Eros incarnate, Alcibiades with his famous good looks is Beauty incarnate (see also the note on 212e). The two of them should have been perfectly matched, and we know from Alcibiades himself that Socrates was brimming with divine treasures, ready to be born (as Diotima would put it) in the kind of attractive medium which Alcibiades could provide (215b, 216e–217a). But Alcibiades could not live up to this high ideal; he could only glimpse the possibilities within Socrates. The only love he can understand is consummated in physical sex. This is the love which enslaves us, and sure enough, as Socrates is Love incarnate, Alcibiades confesses that he is a slave to his love for Socrates (219e).

Alcibiades epitomizes the sensual indulgence we have to give up if we choose Diotima's path, but Plato has given us a portrait of a flesh-and-blood historical figure, not just a moral caricature. His drunken speech makes us smile, but it is a nervous smile, unsure of its ground. It is unclear whether we are laughing with him or at him. The dialogue ends with Socrates trying to convince the comic poet Aristophanes and the tragic poet Agathon that anyone who is expert at one of these two professions should also be expert at the other. It is probable (see the note on 223d) that Plato means us to look back over *Symposium* and conclude that he is himself a writer who combines both skills. If Alcibiades makes us smile, he is also a tragic figure. He is blessed with all the qualities a potential philosopher in the Diotimic mould might require, and above all with enough erotic energy to carry him (we are supposed to feel) as far up Diotima's ladder of love as he may choose to go. But he wastes it.

If we sympathize with Alcibiades, that is because we can recognize ourselves in him. Skilfully, then, Plato leaves us not with the remote mysteries Diotima outlined (though they remain as a distant beacon), but with a human portrait with which we can identify. He wants us to think that we, like Alcibiades, are at the foot of Diotima's ladder, and that it is up to us whether we start to climb it.

SELECT BIBLIOGRAPHY

This is a select bibliography in three main senses. It lists only works written in English, only a small proportion of those that are known to me (a few more are mentioned where appropriate in the notes), and only those I judge likely to be most useful to Greekless readers. I do not agree with all of any of the works mentioned, but they are the best of their kind, in my opinion, and will therefore best help the reader pursue and deepen his or her interests in *Symposium*.

Translations

Four previous translations are worth mentioning:

Hamilton, W., *Plato, The Symposium* (Harmondsworth: Penguin, 1951).

Although slightly old-fashioned, Hamilton's version does not suffer from the over-translation which tends to characterize:

Nehamas, A., and Woodruff, P., *Plato, Symposium* (Indianapolis: Hackett, 1989).

Less easy to obtain, but also containing valuable essays by J. Brentlinger, is:

Groden, S. Q., *The Symposium of Plato* (Amherst: University of Massachusetts Press, 1970).

Useful especially for its wide-ranging commentary is:

Allen, R. E., *The Dialogues of Plato*, ii. *The Symposium* (New Haven, Conn.: Yale University Press, 1991).

Editions

These are both scholarly works, and include the Greek text:

Bury, R. G., *The Symposium of Plato*, 2nd edn. (Cambridge: Cambridge University Press, 1932).

Dover, K. J., *Plato, Symposium* (Cambridge: Cambridge University Press, 1980).

Plato in General

Plato is set in his general ancient philosophical context with admirable concision by:

SELECT BIBLIOGRAPHY

Irwin, T., *Classical Thought* (Oxford: Oxford University Press, 1989).

Among the many books on Plato, the following may be recommended for readers of *Symposium*:

Grube, G. M. A., *Plato's Thought* (London: Methuen, 1935).
Hare, R. M., *Plato* (Oxford: Oxford University Press, 1982).
Rankin, H. D., *Plato and the Individual* (London: Methuen, 1964).

Symposia

An excellent collection of essays on all aspects of the phenomenon is:

Murray, O. (ed.), *Sympotica: A Symposium on the Symposion* (Oxford: Oxford University Press, 1990).

Homosexuality

The essential book on the subject is:

Dover, K. J., *Greek Homosexuality* (London: Duckworth, 1978).

Date

The date of Plato's composition of the dialogue has been discussed in:

Dover, K. J., 'The Date of Plato's *Symposium*', *Phronesis*, 10 (1965), 2–20.
Mattingly, H. B., 'The Date of Plato's *Symposium*', *Phronesis*, 3 (1958), 31–9.

Dover's article, which is in part a reply to Mattingly, is now taken to be authoritative.

The Dialogue as a Whole

There are valuable surveys of the whole dialogue, or broad features of it, in:

Guthrie, W. K. C., *A History of Greek Philosophy*, iv. *Plato, The Man and His Dialogues: Earlier Period* (Cambridge: Cambridge University Press, 1975).
Markus, R. A., 'The Dialectic of Eros in Plato's *Symposium*', *Downside Review*, 73 (1955), 219–30; repr. in G. Vlastos (ed.), *Plato: A Collection of Critical Essays*, ii (Garden City, NY: Anchor Books, 1971), 132–43.

Because thought and action are more closely interwoven in *Symposium* than in any other work of Plato's, the dialogue has attracted a number of interpretations which rely more on the drama than on the philosophy. Of these, the following may be mentioned:

Dorter, K., 'The Significance of the Speeches in Plato's *Symposium*', *Philosophy and Rhetoric*, 2 (1969), 215–34.

Penwill, J. L., 'Men in Love: Aspects of Plato's *Symposium*', *Ramus*, 7 (1978), pp. 143–75.

Wolz, H. G., 'Philosophy as Drama: An Approach to Plato's *Symposium*', *Philosophy and Phenomenological Research*, 30 (1969/70), 323–53.

The narrative form of the dialogue, its purposes, and its relation to the philosophy, are interestingly discussed in:

Halperin, D. M., 'Plato and the Erotics of Narrativity', in J. C. Klagge and N. D. Smith (eds.), *Methods of Interpreting Plato and His Dialogues* (Oxford: Oxford University Press, 1992), 93–129.

The First Five Speeches

Although they invariably also take account of the place of the individual speeches in the dialogue as a whole, there have been useful studies of some of the first five speeches on love:

Dover, K. J., 'Eros and Nomos (Plato, *Symposium* 182a–185c)', *Bulletin of the Institute of Classical Studies*, 11 (1964), 31–42.

—— 'Aristophanes' Speech in Plato's *Symposium*', *Journal of Hellenic Studies*, 86 (1966), 41–50.

Edelstein, L., 'The Role of Eryximachus in Plato's *Symposium*', *Transactions of the American Philological Association*, 75 (1945), 85–103; repr. in L. Edelstein, *Ancient Medicine* (Baltimore: Johns Hopkins University Press, 1971), 153–71.

Konstan, D., and Young-Bruehl, E., 'Eryximachus' Speech in the *Symposium*', *Apeiron*, 16 (1982), 40–6.

Neumann, H., 'On the Sophistry of Plato's Pausanias', *Transactions of the American Philological Association*, 94 (1964), 261–7.

—— 'On the Comedy of Plato's Aristophanes', *American Journal of Philology*, 87 (1966), 420–26.

Alcibiades' Speech

Two studies which use Alcibiades' speech as the starting-point for discussion of the dialogue or some aspects of it are:

Gagarin, M., 'Socrates' Hybris and Alcibiades' Failure', *Phoenix*, 31 (1977), 22–37.

Nussbaum, M. C., 'The Speech of Alcibiades: A Reading of Plato's *Symposium*', *Philosophy and Literature*, 3 (1979), 131–72; rev. and repr. as ch. 6 (pp. 165–99) of M. C. Nussbaum, *The Fragility of Goodness* (Cambridge: Cambridge University Press, 1986).

Nussbaum's reading of the dialogue is very striking and contentious, so (as well as Gill's paper below) see:

Price, A. W., 'Martha Nussbaum's *Symposium*', *Ancient Philosophy*, 11 (1991), 285–99.

Alcibiades' speech is also used as a source for understanding Socrates' habitual irony in a typically brilliant and controversial essay by:

Vlastos, G., 'Socratic Irony', *Classical Quarterly* 37 (1987), 79–96; repr. in H. H. Benson (ed.), *Essays on the Philosophy of Socrates* (Oxford: Oxford University Press, 1992), 66–85.

Plato's Own Theory of Love

There are three excellent (though differing) book-length accounts of Plato's views in *Symposium* and other dialogues:

Gould, T., *Platonic Love* (London: Routledge & Kegan Paul, 1963).

Price, A. W., *Love and Friendship in Plato and Aristotle* (Oxford: Oxford University Press, 1989).

Santas, G. X., *Plato and Freud: Two Theories of Love* (Oxford: Basil Blackwell, 1988).

Of these, the first is rather less scholarly (though no less learned) and therefore rather more readable than the other two. A very influential paper, which criticized Plato's theory as insensitive and egoistical, and which has coloured all subsequent work on the subject, is:

Vlastos, G., 'The Individual as an Object of Love in Plato', in G. Vlastos, *Platonic Studies*, 2nd edn. (Princeton, NJ: Princeton University Press, 1981), 3–42.

The metaphysics and methodology of the famous 'ascent' passage (210a–212a) are discussed in:

Chen, L. C. H., 'Knowledge of Beauty in Plato's *Symposium*', *Classical Quarterly*, 33 (1983), 66–74.

Moravcsik, J. M. E., 'Reason and Eros in the "Ascent"-Passage of the *Symposium*', in J. P. Anton and G. L. Kustas (eds.), *Essays in*

SELECT BIBLIOGRAPHY

Ancient Greek Philosophy (Albany: State University of New York Press, 1971), 285–302.

Stannard, J., 'Socratic Eros and Platonic Dialectic', *Phronesis*, 4 (1959), 120–34.

The unusual claim that Diotima's speech does *not* reflect Plato's own views is argued by:

Neumann, H., 'Diotima's Concept of Love', *American Journal of Philology*, 86 (1965), 33–59.

Some long-standing misconceptions are cleared up with admirable clarity by:

White, F. C., 'Love and Beauty in Plato's *Symposium*', *Journal of Hellenic Studies*, 109 (1989), 149–57.

Other important papers on Plato's theory of love in whole or in part are:

Cornford, F. M., 'The Doctrine of Eros in Plato's *Symposium*', in F. M. Cornford, *The Unwritten Philosophy and Other Essays* (Cambridge: Cambridge University Press, 1950), 68–80; repr. in G. Vlastos (ed.), *Plato: A Collection of Critical Essays*, ii (Garden City, NY: Anchor Books, 1971), 119–31.

Cummings, P. W., 'Eros as Procreation in Beauty', *Apeiron*, 10 (1976), 23–8.

Gill, C., 'Platonic Love and Individuality', in A. Loizou and H. Lesser (eds.), *Polis and Politics* (Aldershot: Avebury, 1990), 69–88.

Halperin, D. M., 'Platonic Eros and What Men Call Love', *Ancient Philosophy*, 5 (1985), 161–204.

Levy, D., 'The Definition of Love in Plato's *Symposium*', *Journal of the History of Ideas*, 40 (1979), 285–91.

Finally, a valuable survey of Platonic thought on the subject, with a convincing attempt to reconcile his apparently divergent comments, can be found in:

Kahn, C. H., 'Plato's Theory of Desire', *Review of Metaphysics*, 44 (1987), 77–103.

PLATO
SYMPOSIUM

The numbers and letters which appear in the margins through-out the translation are the standard means of precise reference to passages in Plato's works. They refer to the pages and sections of pages of the edition of Plato by Stephanus (Henri Estienne), published in Geneva, 1578.

I have translated the Greek text of J. Burnet's Oxford Classical Text, except in the few places indicated in the notes.

APOLLODORUS: I think I'm quite an expert in what 172a
you're asking about.* I mean, just the other day I was
on my way up to town from my home in Phalerum*
and an acquaintance of mine spotted me from behind
and called out to me—he was some way off. He used
his raised voice as an opportunity to have a bit of
fun:* 'Hey you!' he shouted. 'You Phalerian there!
Apollodorus! Wait for me, won't you?'

I stopped and waited for him to catch up. 'You
know, Apollodorus,' he said, 'I was looking for you
only the other day. I wanted to ask you what happened
at that party which Agathon, Socrates, Alcibiades, and b
all the other guests were at, and to find out how their
speeches on love went. I've already had a report from
someone else (who'd been told about it by Phoenix the
son of Philip), but his account wasn't very clear. He did
mention, though, that you knew about it as well. So
please will you tell me? I mean, Socrates is your friend,
so it's perfectly appropriate for you to report what he
says. But tell me first', he added, 'whether or not you
were actually there when they met.'

'It certainly looks as though you've heard a garbled
version of the story,' I said, 'if you're under the im- c
pression that the party you're asking about took place
a short while ago, and so that I could have been there.'

'Yes, I did think that,' he said.

'But how could I have been, Glaucon?' I asked.
'Agathon hasn't lived here in Athens for many years,
you know, and it's less than three years since I've been
among Socrates' companions and have been making
it my business to know, day by day, what he says
and does. It's only been that long since I stopped my
pointless running around. I used to think I was getting 173a
somewhere, when I was worse off than anyone—well,

3

just as badly off as you are now, since you'd rather do anything than do philosophy.'

'Don't tease,' he said. 'Just tell me, please, when it was that they *did* all meet.'

'When you and I were still boys,' I replied. 'Agathon had won with his first tragedy, and they met on the day after he and the cast had performed the victory rites.'*

'It really was a long time ago, then,' he said. 'But who told you the story? Was it Socrates himself?'

b 'Oh, good heavens, no!' I exclaimed. 'It was the same person who told Phoenix about it. He's called Aristodemus—from the deme of Cydathenaeum, a little fellow, never wears shoes.* He'd been there at the party, since he was one of the greatest lovers* Socrates had at the time, I think. All the same, I did also ask Socrates later about some of what Aristodemus told me, and the two accounts coincided.'

'Why don't you go through it for me, then?' he asked. 'There's absolutely nothing on the road to Athens to stop travellers talking and listening to one another.'

So we talked as we walked, and that's why, as I said at c the beginning, I'm quite an expert. If I've got to go through it all for you too, so be it. Besides, I've found in the past that I get an immense amount of pleasure from discussing philosophy myself or listening to others doing so; I don't even stop to think how much good it's doing me as well. But other types of discussion make me cross, especially the kind you affluent businessmen have. I feel sorry for you, my friends, because you think you're getting somewhere when you're actually getting d nowhere. I imagine that by your lights I'm in a bad way, and I suppose you're right—but I don't *suppose* what you are, I *know* it for sure!

COMPANION: You never change, Apollodorus: you put yourself and others down all the time. I get the impression that you regard literally everyone, from yourself onwards, as unhappy—except Socrates. I've no idea how on earth you came to get your nickname 'the softy',* since your conversational tone is invariably the

PROLOGUE

one you're displaying now, of impatience with yourself
and everyone else—except Socrates.

APOLLODORUS: So if I think this way about myself e
and about you, then I must be raving mad—is that it,
my friend?

COMPANION: We oughtn't to quarrel about this
now, Apollodorus. Couldn't you just stick to what we
asked you and describe their speeches?

APOLLODORUS: All right, then. They went something like this ... But it might be better for me to try to
tell you the whole story right from the start, which is 174a
how Aristodemus told it to me. He said that he happened
to meet Socrates under unusual circumstances—bathed
and wearing shoes!* He asked him where he was going,
all smartened up like that.

'I'm going to dinner at Agathon's,' Socrates replied.
'You see, I didn't like the look of the crowd yesterday
at the victory celebration, so I kept away from him
there; but I promised to be there today. That's why I've
tricked myself out: he's good-looking, and I must look
good when I visit him. What about you?' he asked.
'How do you feel about coming to a dinner uninvited?
Would you be prepared to do that?'   b

'Whatever you say,' Aristodemus replied.

'Come with me, then,' Socrates said, 'and we'll distort
and alter the proverb, to show that in fact "Good men
go of their own accord to *good* men's feasts".* I mean,
Homer's not far off actually brutalizing the proverb,
let alone distorting it: in his poem Agamemnon is an
exceptionally good man—good at warfare—and Menelaus is a "feeble fighter",* yet when Agamemnon is c
performing a ritual sacrifice and hosting a celebration,
Homer has Menelaus coming uninvited to the feast—a
worse man to a better man's feast.'

In response to this Aristodemus said, 'Actually, I
too may fit the Homeric situation rather than the one
you're imagining, Socrates, since I'm of no consequence
and I'm going uninvited to a clever man's feast. So
you'd better think up an excuse for bringing me, because

5

I won't admit to coming uninvited: I'll tell them you
d invited me!'

'"The two of us travelling together up the road"* will
plan our lines,' Socrates replied. 'Let's go.'

The conversation went something like that, and then
they set off. Now, as Socrates was walking along, he
started mulling something over in his mind and began to
lag behind. Aristodemus waited for him, but Socrates
told him to go on ahead. When Aristodemus arrived at
e Agathon's house, he found the door open, and was
immediately in a rather embarrassing situation: one of
the house-slaves received him and took him straight
through to the dining-room, where he found the others
on their couches just about to start eating. As soon
as Agathon spotted him, he said, 'Aristodemus, what
perfect timing! You can join us for dinner. If you've
come for any other reason, please put it off for now. I
was looking for you yesterday, in fact, to give you an
invitation, but I couldn't find you. But why haven't you
brought us Socrates?'

I turned around, said Aristodemus, but Socrates was
nowhere to be seen behind me. So I explained that I *had*
come with Socrates, since he'd invited me to dinner
there.

'Well, I'm glad you're here,' said Agathon. 'But where
is Socrates?'

175a   'He was behind me a moment ago, on his way into the
house; I can't think where he could have got to either.'

Agathon sent a slave to go and look for Socrates and
bring him in, and suggested that Aristodemus share
Eryximachus' couch.* A slave washed him so that he
could take his place on the couch,* and then another
slave came with news of Socrates: 'He's out there. He's
turned off into our neighbours' porch and is standing
there. I invited him in, but he refused.'

'How odd!' said Agathon. 'Why don't you invite him
again? And don't take no for an answer.'

b   'No,' Aristodemus said, 'leave him be. He tends to do
that sometimes—to just turn aside and stop, wherever

he might be. I'm sure he'll come soon. So don't disturb him, but leave him be.'

'All right. If you say so, that's what we'll do,' said Agathon. 'But you slaves, the rest of us will start eating now, please. You generally serve whatever you like when no one's overseeing you—and I've never done that. So now treat me and the rest of these people here as your dinner-guests, and attend to our needs. Make us proud of you!'

c

They then started dinner, Aristodemus said, but Socrates still didn't come into the house. Agathon was often on the point of telling a slave to fetch Socrates, but Aristodemus stopped him. And Socrates as usual turned up before too long; at the most, they were about halfway through dinner.

Now, Agathon happened to have the end couch to himself,* so he said, 'Come here, Socrates, and share my couch. It'll do me good to get close to you—I'll come into contact with whatever piece of wisdom occurred to you out there in the porch. You obviously d found what you were looking for, because you wouldn't have given up until you had, so it's yours now.'

Socrates sat down and said, 'Wouldn't it be nice if wisdom was like that, Agathon? Imagine if it could flow by contact from someone who had more of it into someone who had less of it! It would be like water flowing along wool from a fuller cup into an emptier one. If wisdom *is* like that, I think it's very important for me to share your couch, since I'm sure I'll get lots of e excellent wisdom from you, until I'm full up. I mean, my wisdom is insignificant, or as untrustworthy as a dream, whereas yours is brilliant and has great potential too, as is proved by the fact that, despite your youth, it shone out so powerfully and clearly the day before yesterday, with thirty thousand Greeks to witness it.'*

'You do treat people brutally, Socrates!' said Agathon. 'Anyway, we'll go to arbitration a little later, you and I, on the question of our wisdom, and make Dionysus

7

our arbiter.* But first things first: why don't you concentrate on dinner for the time being?'

176a So Socrates lay down on the couch. Once he and
everyone else had finished eating, they performed all
the traditional rites—the libations, the hymns to Zeus,
and so on—and then they turned to drinking. Pausanias
broke the silence by speaking more or less as follows:
'Now, gentlemen, what's the easiest way for us to go
about our drinking? I have to tell you that I'm really in
a pretty bad state from yesterday's drinking, and I
could do with a break. I think the same goes for most
of the rest of you as well, since you were there yesterday.
So what do you think? How can we best make our
b drinking easy on ourselves?'

'Good thinking, Pausanias,' said Aristophanes. 'We
must do everything we can to soften the effect of our
drinking. I speak as one of those who was soused
yesterday.'

After this interchange, Eryximachus the son of Acu-
menus spoke up: 'You're quite right,' he said. 'And I'd
like to ask one of you in particular whether he's fit
enough for drinking . . . Well, Agathon?'

'No, I'm certainly not up to it either,' Agathon replied.

c Eryximachus said, 'What a blessing for us—me,
Aristodemus, Phaedrus, and these people here—that
you professional drinkers are in no state to carry on,
because we're never up to it. I'm not counting Socrates,
since he's ready for either alternative: whichever of
the two courses we follow will be all right with him.
Anyway, since no one here seems inclined to drink a lot
of wine, then you might not mind so much if I tell
you the truth about getting drunk. If practising as a
d doctor has made one thing plain to me, I'd say it's that
drunkenness is bad for people. If it were up to me,
then, I wouldn't want to have much to drink, and I
wouldn't recommend it to anyone else either, especially
if he's still hung over from the day before!'

Phaedrus of Myrrhinus came in at this point,
Aristodemus said. 'Well,' he said, 'I usually follow your

8

advice, especially in medical matters, and everyone else will as well in the present instance, if they're thinking straight.'

At this, everyone agreed not to make the party a e drunken one, but to drink only for pleasure.

'Now that we've decided that the amount anyone drinks is his own choice, without there being any external compulsion,'* Eryximachus said, 'my next suggestion is that the pipe-girl who's just come in is allowed to go; she can play for herself or, if she prefers, for the women in their quarters.* But today let's spend our time together in conversation. On what topic? I'll gladly propose one, if you want.'

That suited everyone, and they told him to make 177a his proposal. So Eryximachus said, 'Let me begin by paraphrasing Melanippe in Euripides' play and say that my proposal is "not my own tale, but comes from Phaedrus here".* You see, Phaedrus occasionally voices a complaint of his to me and says, "Isn't it shocking, Eryximachus, that just about the only god the poets have failed to compose hymns and paeans to is Love? Such a venerable and important god, and not one of all the many poets there have been has ever composed a single encomium to him.* Then again, look at how the b worthy sophists write eulogies in prose to Heracles and so on, as the incomparable Prodicus has, for instance* . . . well, that may not be too surprising, but I've actually before now come across a book, by a clever author,* which included an extraordinary accolade to the usefulness of salt! And one can find plenty of eulogies of other similar things. Imagine people devoting c all that time and effort to things of this order, while the kind of praise Love deserves has never up to now been undertaken by anyone. So important a god, and so little attention has been paid to him!" Now, I think Phaedrus is right, so I'd like to make a donation, as a favour to him, and at the same time I think it's right that those of us who are here should take this opportunity to glorify the god. If you agree, then, the d spoken word should be perfectly adequate for us, as a means of passing the time. I think each of us ought to make the best speech in praise of Love he can, moving around the couches from left to right and starting with Phaedrus, since he has the first couch and is also the prime mover of the topic.'

'Your proposal will be carried unanimously, Eryximachus,' Socrates said. '*I*'m certainly not going to argue against it—I with my claim that the ways of love are all I understand.* Agathon and Pausanias surely

e won't object,* and neither will Aristophanes, since Dionysus and Aphrodite are all he's ever occupied with.* I can't see anyone else here who's likely to object either. I would like to point out that the arrangement isn't fair on those of us whose couches come last, but we won't complain, as long as the earlier speakers do their job well enough. So we wish Phaedrus all the best for the opening speech; let's hear his eulogy of Love!'

Socrates' words met with universal approval and everyone joined him in telling Phaedrus to start. Now,

178a Aristodemus couldn't quite remember every detail of everyone's speeches, and *I* don't remember everything *he* told me either. But I'll give you a pretty accurate report of what he remembered of each speech, at least of the aspects which have stuck in my mind.

So, as I say, he said that Phaedrus spoke first. Phaedrus began somewhat as follows: 'We should look to Love's origins to see one of the chief reasons why both men and gods find him a great and awesome god. The point

b is that he is venerated as a primordial god, as is proved by the fact that no layman, and no poet either, assigns Love parents. Hesiod* says that Chaos came first, "and then broad-breasted Earth, to be a safe seat for all, and Love". Acusilaus agrees with Hesiod, and Parmenides says about Love's origins, "The very first of all the

c gods she devised was Love."* So there's wide assent that Love is a primordial god.

'It's because he's primordial that he's responsible for

10

some of our greatest benefits. I mean, the greatest benefit, to my mind, that a young man can come by in his youth is a virtuous lover,* and a virtuous boyfriend is just as good for a lover too. Anyone who wants to live a good life needs to be guided throughout his life by something which love imparts more effectively than family ties can, or public office, or wealth, or anything else. What is this "something"? The ability to feel shame d at disgraceful behaviour and pride in good behaviour, because without these qualities no individual or community could achieve anything great or fine.

'Imagine a man in love having some disgraceful action of his discovered, or being detected in a cowardly failure to defend himself against being made to accept some indignity. My claim is that being found out by his boyfriend would cause him more distress than being found out by his father, his friends, or anyone else. e And the same evidently goes for the boyfriend: he feels particularly ashamed at being caught behaving badly by his lovers. The best conceivable organization (supposing it were somehow possible) for a community or a battalion would be for it to consist of lovers and their boyfriends,* since they'd compete with one another in avoiding any kind of shameful act. It's hardly an exaggeration to say that a handful of such men, fighting 179a side by side, could conquer the whole world.* I mean, it goes without saying that the last person a lover wants to be seen by, in the act of deserting or throwing away his weapons, is his boyfriend; however many times he had to choose, he'd rather die than that. And as for abandoning his boyfriend or not helping him when danger threatens—well, possession by Love would infuse even utter cowards with courage and make them indistinguishable from those to whom bravery comes most easily. The effect that Love has on lovers is exactly what Homer described, when he talked about a b god "breathing might" into some hero or other.*

'Moreover, only lovers are prepared to sacrifice themselves—and this goes for women as well as for

11

men. The Greek world has been given sufficient proof of this by Pelias' daughter Alcestis, who was the only one prepared to die for her husband, even though his parents

c were alive. Thanks to her love, she was so much more loyal than his parents that she made them seem related to their son in name alone, and otherwise to come from a different family. Men and gods approved so much of this action of hers that although there have been many noble deeds and many performers of them, and although the gods have awarded only a very few of these people the privilege of having one's soul come back up from Hades, they let hers come back, because they were so

d impressed with what she'd done. That's how highly even the gods value the dedication and courage of love.

'They sent Orpheus the son of Oeagrus away from Hades unsatisfied, however: they showed him only a phantom of his wife (whom he'd come to fetch), but refused to give him the real thing, because they regarded him as soft—after all, he was a musician—and, to their mind, he hadn't been brave enough to die for his love as Alcestis had, but had found a way to enter Hades while still alive. And this explains why they punished him, and had him die at the hands of women,

e whereas they rewarded Achilles the son of Thetis by letting him go to the Isles of the Blessed.*

'The reason was that although Achilles found out from his mother that his killing of Hector would cause his own death, and that if he avoided doing this he'd go home and die of old age, he was brave enough to stand by his lover Patroclus* and to avenge him—he

180a didn't choose just to die *for* Patroclus, but even to die *as well as* him, since Patroclus was already dead. Now, Aeschylus is talking nonsense when he claims* that Achilles was Patroclus' lover: Achilles was more attractive than Patroclus—in fact he was the most attractive hero there was—and was still beardless. He was also much younger than Patroclus, as Homer records.* Anyway, while it's true that there is no courage which the gods value more highly than the courage of love, they are more amazed and impressed by, and more b generous towards, a loved one's affection for a lover than a lover's for his boyfriend, since a lover is possessed by a god and therefore in a more godlike state than his beloved. *That*'s why they honoured Achilles more than Alcestis by letting him go to the Isles of the Blessed.

'So, as I say, Love is one of the most ancient and venerated gods, and one of the most effective in helping a person, during his lifetime or after it, attain goodness and happiness.'

That was more or less how Phaedrus' speech went. c Several other speeches followed which Aristodemus couldn't quite remember, so he left them out and reported Pausanias' speech next. It went like this: 'I think there's a problem with the topic we've been set, Phaedrus, in that we've been told to speak in unqualified praise of Love. That would be fine if Love were uniform, but in fact he isn't, and given that he isn't, it would be better to begin by defining which kind of Love we have to praise. So what I'll try to do is set things straight by d first stating which Love deserves our praise, and then delivering the kind of eulogy the god deserves.

'As we all know, Love and Aphrodite are inseparable. Now, if Aphrodite were uniform, so would Love be; but she is twofold and so, inevitably, Love is twofold too. The duality of Aphrodite is undeniable: one Aphrodite— the one we call Celestial—is older and has no mother, though her father is Uranus; the other, the younger one, is the daughter of Zeus and Dione, and is called Common.* It follows, therefore, that the same distinction e of title—Common and Celestial—should be applied to the different Loves who are the associates of one or the other Aphrodite.

'Now, every single god deserves our praise, but we do have to try to distinguish these two Loves' respective domains. The point is that it is in the nature of every action to be, in itself, neither right nor wrong. Look at what we're doing now, for instance. We could either be 181a drinking or singing or talking. None of these is right in itself: the outcome depends on the doing, on how each of them is done. If it is done well and properly, it is right; if it is done badly, it is wrong. The same goes for loving and for Love, then: only the Love who incites us to love properly is good and deserves our praise.*

'Now, the Love who accompanies Common Aphrodite
b is certainly common, and his effects are totally random; this is the Love which ordinary people experience. In the first place, they love women as well as boys; secondly, when they do fall in love, they're attracted to the bodies rather than the minds of the people they love; thirdly, the reason they're attracted to the most unintelligent people imaginable* is that all they're after is the satisfaction of their desires and they don't care whether or not those desires are *properly* satisfied. That's why their activities in this sphere are random: it's all the same to them whether their behaviour is good or bad. The point is that, of the two goddesses, their Love stems from the
c one who is far less mature and who is also, thanks to her parentage, partly male and partly female.

'On the other hand, the Love who accompanies Celestial Aphrodite is wholly male, with no trace of femininity.* (This, then, is the Love which is for boys, and a second point to note is that the provenance of this Love is the goddess who is older and incapable of treating people brutally.)* That is why this Love's inspiration makes people feel affection for what is inherently stronger and more intelligent—which is to say that it makes people incline towards the male.

'A further distinction can be made among men who are sexually attracted towards boys: only some are
d motivated by a pure form of Celestial Love, in the sense that they don't have affairs with boys who are younger than the age at which intelligence begins to form, which more or less coincides with when they begin to grow a beard. It seems to me that not having affairs until then is a sign that one is ready to enter into a lifelong relationship and partnership, as opposed to intending to dupe the

14

boy by getting on friendly terms with him while he's still young and foolish, and then scornfully abandoning him and running off to someone else.*

'There even ought to be a law against having affairs with young boys, to prevent all that time and effort e being spent on an unpredictable matter. I mean, there's no telling how boys are going to turn out—whether their minds or their bodies will end up good or bad. Now, good men make this rule of their own accord for themselves and are glad to do so, but a rule like this has to be imposed on the common run of lover; it's no different from how we also prevent them, as best we can, from having affairs with free-born women. There are people who go so far as to maintain that it's 182a disgusting to gratify a lover—a slur for which these common lovers are responsible. It arises when people look at these common lovers and see their inopportune and immoral behaviour;* I mean, their behaviour—any behaviour—wouldn't warrant criticism, surely, if it were moderate and within the guidelines of convention.

'Now, in most states, it's easy to grasp the conventions that govern love, since they have been defined in a straightforward manner; but here and in Sparta* the matter is complex. In Elis and Boeotia and other places b where rational argument is not their forte, the rule is straightforward: it's acceptable to gratify a lover, and no one of any age would cast aspersions on it. I imagine that this helps them—given that they're useless at arguing—to avoid all the bother of trying to persuade the lads. However, the notion that it's wrong is widespread in Ionia and elsewhere in the Persian empire.* It's because they're ruled by tyrants that the Persians condemn it, and higher education and sport as well—the reason being, I suppose, that it's not in the c rulers' interests to have their subjects cultivate ambition or the kind of firm loyalty and friendship which Love is particularly good at engendering. In fact, this was the lesson our local Athenian tyrants learned too, since it was Aristogiton's love and the constancy of Harmodius' loyalty which caused the downfall of the tyrants.*

   'In other words, wherever gratifying a lover is pro-
d scribed, this is due to the proscribers' corruption (in the
form of the rulers' greed and the subjects' cowardice),
and wherever it is straightforwardly accepted, this is due
to mental sluggishness on the part of the rule-makers.
Our Athenian customs, however, are far from being
flawed in these ways; they are also, as I say, not easy to
comprehend, if you think about them. For example, an
overt affair is considered to be better than a clandestine
one, especially if the affair is between people whose
birth and virtue are outstanding (though they may not
be particularly good-looking); again, a lover receives an
incredible amount of encouragement from all quarters,
which implies that there's nothing wrong in what he's
doing; people applaud his conquests and deride his
e defeats; while he's *trying* to make a conquest, society
sanctions approval of the most extraordinary actions on
a lover's part—actions which ... well, if anyone else
were to dare to behave in these ways in pursuit of any
183a other object, with any other goal in mind, he would earn
unmitigated disapproval.* Imagine, for instance, that a
person wanted someone to give him some money, or
wanted to gain political office or some other form
of authority, and imagine that he was prepared to
behave in the kinds of ways lovers behave towards their
boyfriends—to beg and beseech for his prayers to be
fulfilled, to make promises under oath, to sleep in the
other's doorway, to take on the kinds of degrading tasks
even slaves wouldn't perform. His friends and enemies
alike would stop him acting like this: his enemies would
b deride his obsequious servility, while his friends would
tell him off and feel ashamed to be his friends. But
people indulge all these actions when they're performed
by someone in love, and society allows him to carry on
without meeting disapproval, which implies that his
objectives are perfectly acceptable. The most peculiar
thing of all, to the normal way of thinking, is that the
only occasion when the gods pardon perjury is when a

lover is the one making the promise. "A promise inspired by passion", as the proverb says, "is no promise at all."

'So it is enshrined within our code that both gods and c men give a lover a completely free rein. From this point of view, then, you might suppose that in our society a relationship between a lover and his boyfriend is perfectly acceptable for both of them. However, when you see that fathers stop lovers talking to their boyfriends by putting attendants in charge of their sons with specific instructions to that effect, and that if a boy's friends catch him being approached by a lover, they call him names, and also that older people don't stop them d calling him names and don't tell them off as if what they were saying was wrong—when you see all this going on, you might change your mind and think that such relationships are completely *un*acceptable here.

'The fact is, to my mind, that the issue is not straight-forward and, as I said at the start, a relationship is neither right nor wrong in itself, but is right if it is conducted properly and wrong if it is conducted badly. A wrong relationship is one which involves the immoral gratification of a bad man, and a good relationship is one which involves the morally sound gratification of a good man.* A lover is bad if he is of the common type, who loves the body rather than the mind. This makes e him inconstant, because there's no constancy in the object of his desires; as soon as the physical bloom that attracted him fades, he "flies away and is gone",* exposing the shabbiness of all his fine words and promises. On the other hand, a lover who loves goodness of character is constant for life, because of the constancy of the object he's been united with.

'Our customs, then, are designed to be a thorough test of the worth of lovers, so that boys can tell which ones 184a to gratify and which ones to avoid. That is why our society encourages lovers to chase their boyfriends, and the boyfriends to run away: this enables us to come to a decision and to find out, as a result of this test, whether a given lover and his beloved are good or bad. And this

17

also explains, in the first place, why prompt submission is considered shameful: convention allows an interlude to occur, which invariably proves to be a good test. In the second place, it explains why it is considered wrong to be won over by money and political power, because
b this is due either to being intimidated and collapsing in the face of bad treatment, or to being seduced by money and political success in the face of good treatment in these respects. The point is that none of these things are regarded as reliable or constant; and besides, they are incapable of forming a foundation for true friendship.

'Our moral code leaves only a single way, then, for it to be right for a boy to gratify his lover. We sanction ... well, just as we found that it was acceptable, without
c being obsequious or reprehensible, for lovers to do anything, however servile, for their boyfriends, so by the same token there's only one form of voluntary slavery left which isn't reprehensible. This is slavery whose aim is goodness. I mean, our society does sanction being prepared to perform services for another person as long as one's intention is that the person being served will enable one to improve in some sense, such as by increasing one's knowledge:* *this* self-imposed slavery is not regarded as demeaning or obsequious.

'If these two sets of rules—the one governing affairs with boys, and the one governing education and im-
d provement in general—are combined, then acceptable conditions are created for a boy to gratify his lover. I mean, if in any meeting between a lover and his boyfriend each has his set of guidelines—the lover appreciating that any service he performs for a boyfriend who gratifies him would be morally acceptable, and the boy appreciating that any favours he does for a man who is teaching him things and making him good would be morally acceptable, the lover capable of increasing wisdom and
e other aspects of goodness, the boy eager to learn and generally to increase his knowledge*—it is only then, when these facets of the moral code coincide, that it

becomes all right for a boy to gratify a lover. Under any
other circumstances, it is wrong.

'There isn't even anything discreditable about being
duped under these circumstances, whereas every other
situation reflects badly on a person whether or not he is
duped. Suppose someone is led by a lover's putative
wealth to gratify him in the hope of making some money 185a
out of it, but his hopes are dashed: the lover turns out to
be poor and he doesn't get any money. It doesn't make
any difference that he doesn't actually gain. It's still
discreditable, because what he is seen to have revealed
about himself is that he'd do anything, however servile,
in the hope of financial gain, and that is not to his credit.
On the same principle, suppose someone is led by a
lover's putative goodness to gratify him in the expectation
of gaining, for his part, moral benefit from the lover's
friendship, but his hopes are dashed: the man turns out
to be a scoundrel and to have no goodness to his name.
Even so, being deceived in this way is all right, because b
the aspect of himself which *he* is seen to have shown is
that he'd gladly do anything and everything for the
sake of moral improvement, and there's nothing more
creditable than that.

'So there's absolutely nothing wrong with gratifying a
lover for the sake of virtue. This is the Love which
belongs with the Celestial goddess. He is Celestial too,
and should be highly prized by communities as well as
by individuals, since he impels a lover to pay a great deal
of serious attention to the question of his own virtue,
and does the same for the boy who is the object of a
lover's affection. Any other kind of love there might be c
stems from the other goddess, the Common one.

'Well, there you are, Phaedrus,' he concluded. 'That's
my contribution on Love. It's the best I can do on the
spur of the moment.'

Once Pausanias had come to a pause (I learn this kind of
rhetorical balancing* from the experts), Aristodemus
said, it was Aristophanes' turn to speak, but he happened

to be having an attack of hiccups—perhaps because of overeating, but there could have been some other cause—and he wasn't capable of making a speech. So d he turned to Eryximachus—the doctor was lying on the next couch along from him—and said, 'Eryximachus, you're the perfect person either to get rid of my hiccups* or to speak instead of me, until I get over them.'

'I'll do both,' Eryximachus replied. 'I'll not only speak instead of you now—and you can have my turn when you've got rid of them—but while I'm giving my speech, if you hold your breath for a long time, the hiccups might stop. If that doesn't work, gargle with some e water. If they're really persistent, find something with which you can tickle your nose and make yourself sneeze; one or two sneezes will get rid of your hiccups, however severe the attack.'

Aristophanes said, 'Please proceed with your speech. I'll do what you say.'

So Eryximachus gave his speech. 'Well,' he said, 'I think what I have to do . . . I mean, Pausanias started well, but the quality had tailed off by the end of his 186a speech, so what I must do is try to round his speech off. I'm sure the distinction between the two kinds of Love is quite right, but Love isn't only a human mental response to physical attractions; he influences a great many other situations and circumstances as well. The body of every creature on earth is pervaded by Love, as every plant is too; it's hardly going too far to say that Love is present in everything that exists. You could say that one of the things I've noticed as a result of practising medicine b professionally is that Love is a great and awesome god who pervades *every* aspect of the lives of men and gods.

'I like to give prominence to the art of medicine, so I'll make it my starting-point. You see, the two kinds of Love are inherent within the body. As everyone recognizes, physical health and physical disease are two different things, dissimilar from each other. Now, where there is dissimilarity between things, there is also dissimilarity between the things they desire and love. The love experienced by a healthy body, therefore, is different from the love experienced by a sick body. Not long ago Pausanias was claiming that it is all right to gratify good people and wrong to gratify self-indulgent people, and c the situation with bodies is precisely analogous: it is not only all right, but even essential, to gratify the good, healthy parts of a body (that's just another way of describing the process of healing, after all), but it's wrong to gratify the bad, diseased parts—in fact a professional doctor ought not to pander to them at all.

'Put briefly, medicine is the science of the ways of Love as they affect bodily filling and emptying.* What it takes to be a true professional is the ability to discern d within these processes which loves are good and which are bad, and then to effect a change so that a body acquires a good love rather than a bad one; that is, an expert knows how to make a body gain a love which it should have, but doesn't, and rid itself of the presence of the other kind. In other words, he should be capable of reconciling extremes of hostility between the bodily elements, and of making them love one another. Now, there is the greatest hostility between opposites such as cold and hot, bitter and sweet, dry and wet, and so on. These were the opposites that our ancestor Asclepius* e was faced with, and once he knew how to make them love and get along with one another, he founded the art of medicine. That's what poets like our friends here say,* and I'm convinced.

'Anyway, as I say, the science of medicine is completely governed by Love, and so are sport and agriculture.* 187a And it takes only a moment's thought to make it perfectly clear that the same goes for music too. This was perhaps what Heraclitus was getting at, though he didn't express himself well, when he said, "Unity coheres by divergence within itself: look at the structural harmony of a bow and a lyre."* Now, the idea that there's divergence within harmony, that harmony could still exist if the components were divergent, is quite

21

absurd; perhaps what he was trying to say was that it's the job of musical expertise to bring about harmony by
b changing a state of divergence between high and low pitch into one where they are in agreement. I mean, it's impossible for high and low pitch to form a harmony, of course, if they are divergent (because harmony is concord, and concord is a kind of agreement, and divergent things can't be in agreement), and it's also impossible to bring about harmony where there is divergence except by inculcating agreement. Consider rhythm, for example, whose components are fast and slow pace: rhythm
c comes into being when its components are brought from a state of divergence into one of agreement. The part that medicine plays in its domain is played by music here: music produces agreement between all these components, and makes them love and get along with one another. Music is, in fact, the science of the ways of Love in the domain of harmony and rhythm.

'Now, Love's ways may be easy to recognize in harmony and rhythm, whose very constitution depends on them, but so far there's no trace here of Love's duality.* But when it's a question of employing rhythm
d and harmony in human life—either creatively (that is to say, in song-writing) or in turning the compositions, with their tunes and tempos, to good account (that is to say, in education)—then it's hard, and skill is required. It comes back to the same idea as before: moderate people, whose love helps people develop moderation, should be gratified, and their love should be cherished. It's their love which is the good Love, the Celestial Love
e who stems from the Muse Celestia.* Polymnia's Love, however, is the Common Love; one has to be careful that the recipients of this Love enjoy the pleasure he has to offer without being made self-indulgent, just as in medicine it is very important to make *proper* use of the desires which are catered for by cookery, so that a person enjoys the pleasure of eating without getting ill. So any activity a human being or a god* might engage in—music, medicine, or anything else—requires one

22

to take both these Loves into the fullest possible consideration, since they will both be there.

'Even the climate depends crucially on them both for 188a
its constitution. When those factors I mentioned a short
while ago—hot, cold, dry, and wet—are under the influence of the moderate Love, there is harmony between
them and they blend into a temperate climate. They
bring rich harvests, and health not just for plants, but
also for men and all other animals; their effects are
innocuous. But when the other Love, the brutal one, gains
control over the weather, then they cause widespread
destruction and harm. I mean, these are the conditions
which lead to creatures and plants contracting epidemics b
and a wide variety of other diseases, because the result of
these factors immoderately encroaching on one another
is frosts, hailstorms, and blight. Given that these factors
are influenced by Love, what we call astronomy is the
science of the ways of Love in the domain of the
movements of the heavenly bodies and in the domain of
climatic conditions.*

'Furthermore, all forms of religious ritual and the
whole province of divination—in other words, all the
ways in which gods and men communicate with one c
another—are solely concerned with the perpetuation or
the cure of love. Sacrilegious behaviour of any kind
towards one's parents (alive or dead) and the gods tends
to be the consequence of failing to gratify the moderate
Love, and of honouring and revering the other one
instead. It is the job of divination, therefore, to watch
out for cases of this Love's influence and to effect a cure.
Divination engineers good relations between gods and
men, because it is the science of the ways of Love in
human affairs, in the sense that it knows which of these d
ways determine religiously correct behaviour.

'So you can see how extremely powerful Love funda-
mentally is, in all his manifestations; it's not going
too far to say that he is omnipotent. But it is the Love
whose fulfilment lies in virtuous, restrained, and moral
behaviour from both gods and men who has the greatest

power, and is the source of all our happiness. It is he who makes it possible for us to interact on good terms with one another and with our divine masters.

e 'Now, it may well be that, for all my good intentions, my eulogy of Love is deficient in a number of respects; if that is the case, Aristophanes, it's up to you to remedy any defects. Of course, you may be planning a quite different kind of eulogy of the god. If so, do please go ahead. After all, your hiccups have stopped.'

189a Now that it was his turn, Aristophanes said, 'Yes, they've stopped all right, but they didn't until I used the sneezing technique. It makes me wonder if my body's moderate side desires sneeze-like noises and tickles!* I mean, the hiccups stopped straight away, as soon as I used the sneezing technique.'

'My dear Aristophanes,' Eryximachus replied, 'you'd better think carefully about what you're doing. If you make jokes just before you deliver a speech, I'll have to watch out for jokes during your speech. That would

b make you your own worst enemy, since you could otherwise speak without interference.'*

Aristophanes laughed and said, 'You're right, Eryximachus. Please consider my comments withdrawn. And please don't watch over my speech. I mean, my worry is not that what I'm about to say might be funny—that would be a bonus and typical of my Muse— but that it might be absurd.'

'You think you can just take a shot at me and then run away, Aristophanes,' Eryximachus said. 'Well, I might let you off, if I feel like it, and if you deliver the kind of circumspect speech you should, given that you may be

c asked to justify yourself afterwards.'

'All right, then, Eryximachus,' Aristophanes said. 'Actually, I *am* planning to adopt a different approach from the one Pausanias and you took in your speeches. It seems to me that people have completely failed to appreciate how powerful Love is; otherwise, they'd have built vast temples and altars in his honour, and

24

would have instituted enormous sacrifices. Instead, what actually happens is that he gets none of this, although he deserves more of it than any other god, since there's no god who looks out for mankind's interests more than Love. He supports us and heals precisely those ills whose d alleviation constitutes the deepest human happiness. So what I'm going to do is try to introduce you to his power, and then you can pass the message on to others.

'The starting-point is for you to understand human nature and what has happened to it.* You see, our nature wasn't originally the same as it is now: it has changed. Firstly, there used to be three human genders, not just two—male and female—as there are nowadays. There was also a third, which was a combination of e both the other two. Its name has survived, but the gender itself has died out. In those days, there was a distinct type of androgynous person, not just the word, though like the word the gender too combined male and female; nowadays, however, only the word remains, and that counts as an insult.*

'Secondly, each person's shape was complete: they were round, with their backs and sides forming a circle.* They had four hands and the same number of legs, and two absolutely identical faces on a cylindrical neck. 190a They had a single head for their two faces (which were on opposite sides), four ears, two sets of genitals, and every other part of their bodies was how you'd imagine it on the basis of what I've said. They moved around in an upright position, as we do today, in either of their two forward directions; and when it came to running, they supported themselves on all eight of their limbs and moved rapidly round and round, just like when acrobats perform that circular manoeuvre where they stick their legs out straight and wheel over and over.

'The reason there were three genders, and the reason they were as they were, is that the original parent of the b male gender was the sun, while that of the female gender was the earth and that of the combined gender was the moon, because the moon too is a combination, of the

25

sun and the earth. The circularity of their shape and of their means of locomotion was due to the fact that they took after their parents.

'Now, their strength and power were terrifying, and they were also highly ambitious. They even had a go at the gods. Homer's story about how Ephialtes and Otus tried to mount up to heaven to attack the gods is really

c about them.* So Zeus and the rest of the gods met in council to try to decide what to do with them. They were in a quandary: they didn't see how they could kill them and blast them out of existence as they had the giants, because that would also do away with the veneration and sacrificial offerings the human race gave them; but they also didn't see how they could let them get away with their outrageous behaviour. After thinking long and hard about it, Zeus said, "I think I can see a way for the human race to exist, but to be weakened enough to start behaving with some moderation. What

d I'm going to do is split every single one of them into two halves; then they'll be weaker, and at the same time there'll be more in it for us because there'll be more of them. They'll walk about upright on two legs. If in our opinion they continue to behave outrageously," Zeus added, "and they refuse to settle down, I'll cut them in half again, and then they'll go hopping around on one leg."

'With these words, he cut every member of the human race in half, just as people cut sorb-apples in half when

e they're going to preserve them, or cut an egg in two with a hair.* Then he told Apollo to twist every divided person's face and half-neck round towards the gash, the idea being that the sight of their own wounds would make people behave more moderately in the future. He also told Apollo generally to heal their wounds. So Apollo twisted their heads around, and pulled the skin together from all over their bodies on to what is now called the stomach (think of purses being closed by draw-strings), leaving only a single opening in the middle of the stomach, which we call the navel, where he tied

the skin up into a knot. Then he smoothed out most of
the wrinkles and fashioned the chest with the help of a   191a
tool like the one shoe-makers use to iron out the wrinkles
in leather they've got on a last; he left a few wrinkles,
however, the ones in the region of the stomach and the
navel, to act as a reminder of what happened all that
time ago.

'It was their very essence that had been split in two, so
each half missed its other half and tried to be with it;
they threw their arms around each other in an embrace and longed to be grafted together. As a result,
because they refused to do anything without their other
halves, they died of starvation and general apathy. If one   b
of a pair died while the other half was left alive, the
survivor went in search of another survivor to embrace,
and it didn't matter to it whether the half that it fell in
with was half of what had originally been a female
whole (it is the half, not the whole, that we nowadays
call female, of course) or of a male whole.*

'Under these circumstances, they were beginning to
die out. Zeus took pity on them, however, and came up
with another ingenious idea: he changed the position of
their genitals round to their fronts. Up until then, their
genitals too had been on the far side of their bodies, and
procreation and birth hadn't involved intercourse with
one another, but with the ground, like cicadas.* So Zeus   c
moved their genitals round to the front of their bodies
and thus introduced intercourse between two human
beings, with the man as the agent of generation taking
place within the woman. His reasons for doing this were
to ensure that, when couples embraced, as well as
male–female relationships leading to procreation and
offspring, male–male relationships would at least involve
sexual satisfaction, so that people would relax, get on
with their work and take care of other aspects of life.

'So that's how, all that time ago, our innate sexual   d
drive arose. Love draws our original nature back together; he tries to reintegrate us and heal the split in our
nature. Turbot-like, each of us has been cut in half,

and so we are human tallies, constantly searching for our counterparts.* Any men who are offcuts from the combined gender—the androgynous one, to use its former name—are attracted to women, and therefore most adulterers come from this group; the equivalent women

e are attracted to men and tend to become adulteresses.* Any women who are offcuts from the female gender aren't particularly interested in men; they incline more towards women, and therefore female homosexuals come from this group.* And any men who are offcuts from the male gender go for males. While they're boys, because they were sliced from the male gender, they fall in love with men, they enjoy sex with men and they like to be embraced by men. These boys are the ones who are

192a outstanding in their childhood and youth, because they're inherently more manly than others. I know they sometimes get called immoral, but that's wrong: their actions aren't prompted by immorality, but by courage, manliness, and masculinity. They incline towards their own characteristics in others. There's good evidence for their quality: as adults, they're the only men who end up in government.*

'Anyway, when they become men, they're sexually

b attracted to boys and would have nothing to do with marriage and procreation if convention didn't override their natural inclinations. They'd be perfectly happy to see their lives out together without getting married. In short, then, men who are sexually attracted to boys, and boys who love their lovers, belong to this group and always incline towards their own innate characteristics.

'Now, when someone who loves boys—or whatever his sexual preferences may be—actually meets his other half, it's an overwhelming experience. It's impossible to describe the affection, warmth, and love they feel for

c each other; it's hardly an exaggeration to say that they don't want to spend even a moment apart. These are the people who form unbroken lifelong relationships together, for all that they couldn't say what they wanted from each other. I mean, it's impossible to believe that it's their sex-life which does this—that sex is the reason they're each so eager and happy to be in the other's company. They obviously have some other objective, which their minds can't formulate; they only glimpse d what it is and articulate it in vague terms.

'Imagine that Hephaestus came with his tools and stood over them as they were lying together, and asked, "What is it that you humans want from each other?" And when they were unable to reply, suppose he asked instead, "Do you want to be so thoroughly together that you're never at any time apart? If that's what you want, I'd be glad to weld you together, to fuse you into a single person, instead of being two separate people, so that e during your lifetime as a single person the two of you share a single life, and then, when you die, you die as a single person, not as two separate people, and you share a single death there in Hades. Think about it: is this your hearts' desire? If this happened to you, would it bring you happiness?" It's obvious that none of them would refuse this offer; we'd find them all accepting it. There wouldn't be the slightest doubt in any of their minds that what Hephaestus had said was what they'd been wanting all along, to be joined and fused with the one they love, to be one instead of two. And the reason for this is that originally that's exactly how we were— whole beings. "Love" is just the name we give to the desire for and pursuit of wholeness.*   193a

'As I say, in times past we were unified, but now we are scattered; Zeus punished us for our crimes in the same way that the Spartans did the Arcadians.* So the worry is that, if we fail to behave towards the gods with moderation, we'll be further divided, and in that mode of existence we'd be no different from those profiles on tombstones, sawn in two down the line of their noses. We'd be half-dice.* That's why it is everyone's duty to encourage others to behave at all times with due reverence towards the gods, since this makes it possible for good rather than bad to come our way, with Love as our b leader and commander. No one should oppose Love, and to get on the wrong side of the gods is to oppose Love. Anyone who has brought Love round to his side will find, as if by chance, the love of his life, which is a rare event at the moment.

'I don't want Eryximachus to treat my speech as a satire and imagine that I'm talking about Pausanias and
c Agathon. It may well be that they do in fact belong to that category and are both inherently masculine; but what I'm saying applies to everyone, both men and women. We human beings will never attain happiness unless we find perfect love, unless we each come across the love of our lives and thereby recover our original nature. In the context of this ideal, it necessarily follows that in our present circumstances the best thing is to get as close to the ideal as possible, and one can do this by finding the person who is his heart's delight. If we want to praise the god who is responsible for our finding this
d person, it is Love we should praise. It is Love who, for the time being, provides us with the inestimable benefit of guiding us towards our complement and, for the future, holds out the ultimate assurance—that if we conduct ourselves with due reverence towards the gods, then he will restore us to our original nature, healed and blessed with perfect happiness.

'There you are, Eryximachus,' Aristophanes said in conclusion. 'It may have been different from yours, but there's my speech on Love. As I said, I'd be grateful if you didn't try to find any humour in it, and then we can listen to all the remaining speakers—or rather to both
e of them, since only Agathon and Socrates are left.'

'All right,' said Eryximachus, 'I'll do as you say. In fact, I really enjoyed your speech. If I didn't know that Socrates and Agathon were experts in the ways of love, I'd be very worried in case the wealth and variety of the speeches we've already heard left them with nothing to say. As things stand, though, I've got no worries.'
194a   'That's because you've already acquitted yourself successfully in the competition, Eryximachus,' said So-

crates. 'If you were in my situation, however, or rather the situation I'm sure I'll find myself in after an excellent speech from Agathon as well, then you'd have plenty to worry about and you'd be as terrified as I am now.'

'You're out to put a spell on me, Socrates,' said Agathon. 'You'd like me to think that the audience has high hopes of a fine speech from me, so that I lose my composure.'

'I'd really have a bad memory, Agathon,' Socrates replied, 'if I thought you'd be thrown by the tiny b audience we constitute after what I've seen of your courage and self-confidence when you got up on stage with your actors in front of a huge audience. You were about to display your own work in front of them too, and you remained completely unruffled.'

'Hang on, Socrates,' Agathon said. 'Surely you don't think that my obsession with the theatre blinds me to the fact that anyone with any sense will find a small number of intelligent people more alarming than a large number of unintelligent people?'

'No, of course not, Agathon,' Socrates replied. 'I'd be c wrong to think you capable of anything uncultured. I'm well aware that you'd take more notice of those of your acquaintances you regard as clever than you would of the general populace. But are you sure that we here *are* clever? After all, we were also there in the theatre, forming part of the general populace. Anyway, if you *did* ever come across clever people, you'd probably be embarrassed to feel that you might be doing something wrong in front of them. Is that what you mean?'

'That's right,' he said.

'But wouldn't you be embarrassed to feel you were doing something wrong in front of the general populace?'

At this point Phaedrus came in and said, 'Agathon d my friend, if you respond to Socrates' questions, he'll stop caring what happens to any of our current concerns. Everything else goes by the board when he has someone to talk to, especially if that someone is attrac-

31

tive. Although I enjoy hearing Socrates talk, I have to think about the eulogy of Love and receive all of your contributions,* in the form of speeches. After the two of you have paid your due to the god, then you can get into a discussion.'

e   'You're right, Phaedrus,' said Agathon. 'There's no reason why I shouldn't get on with my speech. I mean, Socrates will have plenty of other opportunities in his life for discussions.

'I'd like to start my speech by explaining the tactics of my speech, before actually turning to my speech.* You see, I think that all the previous speakers weren't really praising the god; they were congratulating the human race on how much they thrive on goods the god con- trives. Nothing has been said, however, about the actual
195a nature of the being who bestows these gifts. But there is only one correct approach in composing a eulogy, whatever the topic, and that is to define what the being who is the subject of the speech is in fact like, and what benefits he is responsible for. Accordingly, the proper tactics for us too, in dealing with Love, are first to praise his nature, and then his gifts.

'My claim—may my words be free of sacrilege and profanity*—is that although all the gods live blessed lives, the bliss of none of them compares with that of Love, since none of them is as attractive or as good as he is. I shall now go on to explain what it is about his nature that makes him so attractive.

'In the first place, Phaedrus, he is the youngest of the
b   gods. He himself provides good evidence for this claim, in that he takes evasive action in the face of old age— and the speed of old age is notorious, at any rate in the sense that it bears down on us with inordinate haste! So it is in Love's nature to loathe old age and to keep well away from it. He is a constant companion of young men and (given the validity of the old saying that like always clings to like) he is therefore young himself. Although I agreed with a great deal of what Phaedrus was saying, I can't accept that Love is more ancient than Cronus and

Iapetus;* my claim is that he is the youngest of the gods and is forever young. I also maintain that if Hesiod and c Parmenides have got their facts right, then Necessity, not Love, is responsible for the things they tell us the gods got up to in ancient times. I mean, all those vicious acts like castration and imprisonment* could never have happened if Love had already been among them; they'd have been on good terms with one another, living in peace, as they do now and have done ever since Love's rule over them began.

'So he is young, and sensitive as well as young. He's never had a poet like Homer, however, to demonstrate d his divine sensitivity. I mean, Homer says that Delusion is a goddess with sensitivity—with sensitive feet, any-way!—in the lines,* "Her feet are so sensitive that she steps over men's heads rather than lighting upon the ground." I think Homer expresses her sensitivity very well, by taking as his evidence the fact that she walks only on something soft, never hard. We can draw on the same evidence for Love's sensitivity too, since he doesn't e even step on men's skulls (which are not particularly soft), let alone on the ground; he lives and moves in the softest environment of all. You see, he makes his home in gods' and men's dispositions and minds—and even then, not indiscriminately in every mind, because he withdraws whenever he encounters a mind with a hard disposition and stays only where he finds one that is soft. He lives, then, in the softest conceivable environ-ment, allowing only the softest matter to touch not just his feet, but his whole self. We are bound to conclude that he is highly sensitive.

'He is very young and very sensitive, then, and fluid 196a in form as well. Otherwise, if he were inflexible, he wouldn't have the ability to adapt himself completely to his environment or to pass through minds and remain imperceptible on his original entry and on his departure. Good evidence for the compatibility and fluidity of his form is provided by his grace, a property which is universally held to belong to Love in particular, in the sense that there is constant warfare between Love and physical awkwardness.

'As for the loveliness of Love's complexion, this is symbolized by his practice of making flowers his home.* Love doesn't settle on a body, a mind, or anything else
b which has no bloom or whose bloom has faded; but a fragrant spot full of flowers—that's where he settles and remains.

'I've said enough about Love's attractions, though plenty more could be said; next I have to discuss his goodness. Most importantly, in all his dealings with gods or with men Love acts fairly and is treated fairly too. For oppression and Love are incompatible, so Love is never dealt with harshly when he's at the receiving
c end, and never acts oppressively either, because everyone is happy to carry out any of Love's commands, and situations which involve agreement and the consent of both parties are defined by "law, society's king"* as just.

'Love is characterized by a high degree of self-discipline, as well as by fairness. Everyone accepts that self-discipline is the control of pleasure and desire, and they also accept that there is no pleasure better than Love. So if pleasures fail to match Love, they are defeated by Love, and Love is in control; and if Love is in control of pleasure and desire, then he is particularly self-disciplined.
d 'As for courage, "not even Ares can withstand Love".* I mean, it wasn't Ares who captured Love, but Love who captured Ares—love of Aphrodite, in the story.* Since a captor is superior to a captive, then if A defeats B, when B is otherwise the bravest in the world, it follows that A is absolutely the bravest in the world.

'So much for the god's justice, self-discipline, and courage; it remains to discuss his wisdom.* Now, it's important to be as thorough as possible here. I like to honour *my* art as much as Eryximachus does his,* so
e I'll start by pointing out that Love is so skilled as a creative poet that he creates other poets, in the sense

34

that Love has only to touch a person and, "however coarse he was before",* he becomes a poet. To cut a long story short, we can fairly take this as evidence that Love is good at all aspects of creativity in the field of education, because you can't give what you don't have and you can't teach what you don't know. Moreover, turning to the creation of living creatures, who could 197a deny that all living creatures are engendered and born by the skill of Love? And are we not aware, where expertise in craft is concerned, that while fame and glory await pupils of this god, obscurity awaits those untouched by him? Besides, it was by following where his desire and love led him that Apollo discovered archery, healing, and prophecy, so this would make Apollo a pupil of Love; and by the same token the b Muses learned music from him, Hephaestus learned metalwork, Athena learned weaving, and Zeus learned "the captaincy of gods and men".* And it follows from this that the gods' concerns only became organized as a result of the birth among them of Love—love of beauty, obviously, because there's no such thing as love of repulsiveness—and that previously, as I said at the start, the gods often behaved in a terrible fashion (as the stories record), under the rule of Necessity. Once Love was born, however, both men and gods began to thrive as a result of their love of beauty.*

'It is my opinion, then, Phaedrus, that Love is himself c without equal in attractiveness and in goodness, and secondly is responsible for similar qualities in others. I am moved to express myself in verse and say that he is the one who causes "peace among men, calm on the open sea undisturbed by breath of air, winds' stillness at the end of day, and sleep for those with cares".* He it is who draws insularity out of us and pours familiarity d into us, by causing the formation of all shared gatherings like ours, by taking the lead in festal, choral, sacrificial rites.* He dispenses mildness and dismisses wildness; he is unsparing of goodwill and unsharing of ill-will. He is gracious and gentle;* adored by the wise, admired by the gods; craved when absent, prized when present. Hedonism, luxury, and sensualism, delight, desire, and eroticism—these are his children. He looks after the good and overlooks the bad. In adversity and uncertainty, for passion and discussion, there is no better

e captain or shipmate or guardian deity; for the whole of heaven and the whole of earth, he is matchless and peerless as governor and guide. Everyone should follow in his train, glorifying him with sweet-sounding hymns, sharing the song he sings to charm the minds of gods and men.

'There you are, Phaedrus,' he said in conclusion. 'That will have to do as my speech in honour of the god. I've tried my best to include some entertaining parts, and at the same time not to overdo the serious parts.'

198a Agathon's speech was greeted with cries of admiration from everyone in the room, Aristodemus said; they thought the young man had done credit to himself and to the god. So Socrates looked at Eryximachus and said, 'Do you still think my earlier anxiety was unfounded, Eryximachus? Don't you think, rather, that I was being prophetic when I claimed a short while ago that Agathon would speak brilliantly and that I'd be at a loss for words?'

'I think that's half right,' Eryximachus replied. 'You *were* being prophetic in your claim that Agathon would give a good speech, but I don't think you'll be lost for words.'

b   'But of course I will, my friend,' said Socrates. 'Who on earth could follow such a fine speech? There was so much to it. I wasn't quite so taken with the rest, but the ending... well, it would be impossible not to be impressed with such elegant vocabulary and phraseology. I was aware that I'd be incapable of achieving anything like such elegance in my speech, and I was so ashamed that I almost beat a hasty retreat. If only there'd been

c somewhere for me to go! Homer has perfectly captured what I was going through. Agathon's speech reminded me of Gorgias, you see, so what I was afraid of was that he would end his speech by sending the head of the formidable orator Gorgias against my speech, which would rob me of my voice and so turn me to stone.*

'That was when I realized what a fool I was to have agreed to join in and deliver a eulogy of Love when it came to my turn, and to have claimed expertise in the d ways of love, when in fact I didn't have the slightest clue about the matter—that is, about how I was supposed to go about this eulogy. I was so naïve that I thought the point of any eulogy was to tell the truth about the subject! I thought that, with the truth before you, you were supposed to select from among the facts the ones that were most to your subject's credit and then present them so as to show him in the best possible light. I was very confident in my ability to give a good speech, on the grounds that I knew the truth about how to deliver eulogies.

'But it now looks as though this isn't the way to deliver a proper eulogy after all. What you do is describe your subject in the most generous and glowing terms, e whether or not there's any truth to them. It needn't bother you if you're making it up. Our assignment apparently means that each of us is to deliver a specious eulogy of Love, rather than actually praise him. I suppose that's why you all go to such extreme lengths to argue for the ascription of qualities to Love—to claim that he is like this and responsible for that. It's to make him look as attractive and perfect as possible—and this 199a is obviously not for the benefit of people who already know the facts, so it must be for those who don't know any better. And yes, your eulogies are indeed attractive— wonderful, in fact.

'But you see, I didn't actually know that this was how to go about a eulogy, and in my ignorance I agreed that I too would deliver one in due course. The promise came from my tongue, then, not my heart,* so let's forget it. I mean, I'm not going to give that kind of eulogy—I can't. Nevertheless, I am prepared to tell the truth, if b you'd be happy with that, but I must do it in my own way, because if I try to compete with your speeches, I'll just make a fool of myself. So, Phaedrus, would you accept that kind of speech as well, one which tells you the truth about Love and lets words* and phrases tumble out in any old order?'

Phaedrus and everyone else told him he could speak in any style he thought appropriate.

'Would you also let me ask Agathon a few small questions, Phaedrus?' Socrates asked. 'Then, once I've got his agreement to certain matters, I'll be in a position to deliver my speech.'

c 'Yes, please do ask him your questions,' Phaedrus replied.

'Well now, Agathon,' Socrates began, as far as Aristodemus could remember, 'I thought the preliminary point you made in your speech, about the importance of showing what Love is like before starting on what he does, was excellent. An admirable starting-point, I thought. Now, basically you did a good and splendid job of describing Love's nature; but I'd also like to ask

d you whether or not it's one of Love's characteristics to stand in relation to something. I'm not asking whether Love is related to some mother or father; it would be ridiculous of me to ask whether Love is *of* a mother or a father in this sense.* No, suppose I'd actually asked my question about "father"—whether or not a father is a father *of* someone. The proper answer, if you wanted to give it, would surely be that a father is a father of a son or a daughter, wouldn't it?'

'Yes, of course,' Agathon replied.

'And the same goes for "mother" as well?'

He agreed again.

e 'Now, if you answer just a few more questions, you'll see what I'm getting at,' Socrates went on. 'Suppose I'd asked, "Well, what is it to be a brother? If you're a brother, are you or are you not the brother of someone?"'

'You are,' Agathon said.

38

'That is, you're the brother of a brother or a sister, aren't you?'

'Yes.'

'Let's hear what you have to say about Love too, then,' Socrates said. 'Does Love love nothing or something?'

'He loves something, of course.'

'Now, don't let on yet *what* Love's object is,' said 200a Socrates, 'but bear it in mind and for the time being tell me only this: when you love something, do you desire it?'

'Yes,' he said.

'If you desire and love something, is it something you have in your possession, or not?'

'It's probably something you don't have,' he answered.

'Never mind probability,' Socrates said. 'Don't you think that any case of desire is *necessarily* desire for something which is lacking? If it isn't lacking, you can't desire it, surely. Personally, Agathon, I'd be astonished b if that wasn't necessarily the case. What about you?'

'I agree,' he said.

'Good. Now, if someone was tall, would he *want* to be tall? If someone was strong, would he want to be strong?'

'No, we've implicitly ruled that out already.'

'Because if someone possesses a certain quality, he can't be lacking it.'

'Exactly.'

'The point is this,' Socrates continued. 'If a strong man wanted to be strong, or a fast runner wanted to be fast, or a healthy person wanted to be healthy . . . You see, someone might look at these particular qualities and others like them and think that people with these attributes and qualities *do* also desire the qualities they c have. That's why I'm arguing the point: I want to be sure we don't get the wrong idea. I mean, if you think about it, Agathon, these people are *bound* currently to have whichever of these qualities they have. There's nothing they can do about it, and so of course it isn't a situation in which desire can play a part. If someone says, "I'm healthy, but I still want health" or "I'm wealthy, but I still want wealth" or in short "I desire what I have", we'll respond by saying, "My friend, you d already have wealth (or health or strength). What you want is to have it in the future as well, because there's nothing you can do about the fact that you've got it at the moment. You'd better watch out in case, when you say that you desire something you currently have, what you actually mean is rather different, that you want what you currently have to continue into the future." He'd have to admit that we're right, wouldn't he?'

Agathon agreed.

'In other words,' said Socrates, 'what he's doing in this situation is loving something which is currently inaccessible to him and not in his possession—that is, the continued presence of his attributes in the future.'

e 'Yes,' he said.

'Therefore this and any other case of desire is desire for something which is inaccessible and absent. If there's something you need, miss, or lack, then that's the kind of thing you can desire and love. Yes?'

'Yes.'

'Let's recapitulate our conclusions,' said Socrates. 'First, love is love *of* something; second, that something is something a person currently lacks.'

201a 'Yes,' he said.

'Now in this context I'd like you to remember something you said about Love in your speech. Shall I remind you? These won't be your exact words, but I think you said that the gods' concerns became organized as a result of their love of things of beauty, since it's impossible to love repellent things. Isn't that more or less what you said?'

'Yes, I did,' Agathon agreed.

'It's a plausible idea, my friend,' Socrates remarked. 'And if it's correct, then it follows that Love loves beauty, not repulsiveness, doesn't it?'

'Yes.'

'And haven't we already concluded that love is for b
things one needs and lacks?'

'Yes,' he said.

'It follows that Love needs and lacks beauty.'*

'Inevitably,' he said.

'Well, would you say that something which lacks
beauty and is entirely without beauty is attractive?'

'Of course not.'

'If this is how things stand, then, do you still maintain
that Love is attractive?'

'It rather looks as though I didn't know what I was
talking about before, Socrates,' confessed Agathon.

'And yet you still gave an attractive speech, Agathon,' c
Socrates said. 'But I've got one more little question
for you. Don't you think that anything good is also
attractive?'*

'Yes, I do.'

'So if Love is lacking in attractive qualities, and
if good things are attractive, then Love lacks good
qualities too.'*

'I can't refute you, Socrates,' Agathon said, 'so I dare
say you're right.'

'No,' said Socrates, 'it's the truth you can't refute, my
dear Agathon. Socrates is a pushover.'

'Anyway, I'll leave you in peace now. But there's an d
account of Love which I heard from a woman called
Diotima, who came from Mantinea and was an expert
in love, as well as in a large number of other areas
too. For instance, on one occasion when the Athenians
performed their sacrificial rites to ward off the plague,
she delayed the onset of the disease for ten years.* She
also taught me the ways of love, and I'll try to repeat for
you what she told me. I'll base myself on the conclusions
Agathon and I reached, but I'll see if I can manage on
my own now.

'As you explained, Agathon, it's important to start
with a description of Love's nature and characteristics, e
before turning to what he does. I think the easiest way

41

for me to do this is to repeat the account the woman from Mantinea once gave me in the course of a question-and-answer session we were having. I'd been saying to her, in my own words, almost exactly what Agathon was just saying to me—that Love is an important god and must be accounted attractive. She used the same arguments I used on him to prove that it actually followed from my own ideas that Love *wasn't* attractive or good.

'"What?" I exclaimed. "Do you mean to tell me, Diotima, that Love is repulsive and bad?"

'"You should be careful what you say," she replied. "Do you think that anything which isn't attractive has to be repulsive?"

202a '"Yes, I certainly do."

'"Do you also think that lack of knowledge is the same as ignorance? Haven't you noticed that there's middle ground between knowledge and ignorance?"

'"What middle ground?"

'"True belief," she replied. "Don't you realize that, as long as it isn't supported by a justification, true belief isn't knowledge (because you must be able to explain what you know), but isn't ignorance either (because ignorance can't have *any* involvement with the truth of things)? In fact, of course, true belief is what I said it was, an intermediate area between knowledge and ignorance."

'"You're right," I said.

b '"Stop insisting, then, that 'not attractive' is the same as 'repulsive', or that 'not good' is the same as 'bad'. And then you'll also stop thinking that, just because— as you yourself have conceded—Love isn't good or attractive, he therefore has to be repulsive and bad. He might fall between these extremes."

'"Still, everyone agrees that he's an important god," I said.

'"Do you mean every expert, or are you counting non-experts too?" she asked.

'"Absolutely everyone."

42

'Diotima smiled and said, "But how could people who deny that he's even a god admit that he's an important c god, Socrates?"

' "Who are you talking about?" I asked.

' "You for one," she said, "and I'm another."

' "How can you say that?" I demanded.

' "Easily," she said, "as you'll see if you answer this question. Don't you think that good fortune and beauty are attributes which belong to every single god? Can you really see yourself claiming that any god fails to be attractive and to have an enviable life?"*

' "No, of course I wouldn't," I said.

' "And isn't it when someone has good and attractive attributes that you call him enviable?"

' "Yes."

' "You've admitted, however, that it's precisely be- d cause Love lacks the qualities of goodness and attractiveness that he desires them."

' "Yes, I have."

' "But it's inconceivable that a *god* could fail to be attractive and good in any respect, isn't it?"

' "I suppose so."

' "Can you see now that you're one of those who don't regard Love as a god?" she asked.

' "What is Love, then?" I asked. "Mortal?"

' "Of course not."

' "What, then?"

' "He occupies middle ground," she replied, "like those cases we looked at earlier; he lies between mortality and immortality."

' "And what does that make him, Diotima?"

' "An important spirit, Socrates. All spirits occupy the middle ground between humans and gods." e

' "And what's their function?" I asked.

' "They translate and carry messages from men to gods and from gods to men. They convey men's prayers and the gods' instructions, and men's offerings and the gods' returns on these offerings. As mediators between the two, they fill the remaining space, and so make

43

the universe an interconnected whole. They enable divination to take place and priests to perform sacrifices and rituals, cast spells, and do all kinds of prophecy and sorcery. Divinity and humanity cannot meet directly; the gods only ever communicate and converse with men (in their sleep or when conscious) by means of spirits. Skill in this area is what makes a person spiritual, whereas skill in any other art or craft ties a person to the material world. There are a great many different kinds of spirits, then, and one of them is Love."

203a

' "But who are his parents?" I asked.

b   ' "That's rather a long story," she replied, "but I'll tell you it all the same.* Once upon a time, the gods were celebrating the birth of Aphrodite, and among them was Plenty, whose mother was Cunning. After the feast, as you'd expect at a festive occasion, Poverty turned up to beg, so there she was by the gate. Now, Plenty had got drunk on nectar (this was before the discovery of wine) and he'd gone into Zeus' garden, collapsed, and fallen asleep. Prompted by her lack of means, Poverty came up with the idea of having a child by Plenty, so she lay with

c him and became pregnant with Love. The reason Love became Aphrodite's follower and attendant, then, is that he was conceived during her birthday party; also, he is innately attracted towards beauty and Aphrodite is beautiful.

' "Now, because his parents are Plenty and Poverty, Love's situation is as follows. In the first place, he never has any money, and the usual notion that he's sensitive and attractive is quite wrong: he's a vagrant, with

d tough, dry skin and no shoes on his feet.* He never has a bed to sleep on, but stretches out on the ground and sleeps in the open in doorways and by the roadside. He takes after his mother in having need as a constant companion. From his father, however, he gets his ingenuity in going after things of beauty and value, his courage, impetuosity, and energy, his skill at hunting (he's constantly thinking up captivating stratagems), his desire for knowledge, his resourcefulness, his lifelong pursuit of education, and his skills with magic, herbs, and words.

'"He isn't essentially either immortal or mortal. Some- e times within a single day he starts by being full of life in abundance, when things are going his way, but then he dies away . . . only to take after his father and come back to life again. He has an income, but it is constantly trickling away, and consequently Love isn't ever destitute, but isn't ever well off either. He also falls between knowledge and ignorance, and the reason for this is as follows. No *god* loves knowledge or desires wisdom, 204a because gods are already wise; by the same token, no one else who is wise loves knowledge. On the other hand, ignorant people don't love knowledge or desire wisdom either, because the trouble with ignorance is precisely that if a person lacks virtue and knowledge, he's perfectly satisfied with the way he is. If a person isn't aware of a lack, he can't desire the thing which he isn't aware of lacking."*

'"But Diotima," I said, "if it isn't either wise people or ignorant people who love wisdom, then who is it?"

'"Even a child would have realized by now that it b is those who fall between wisdom and ignorance," Diotima said, "a category which includes Love, because knowledge is one of the most attractive things there is, and attractive things are Love's province. Love is bound, therefore, to love knowledge, and anyone who loves knowledge is bound to fall between knowledge and ignorance. Again, it's the circumstances of his birth which are responsible for this feature of his, given that his father is clever and resourceful and his mother has neither quality.

'"There you are, then, my dear Socrates: that's what Love is like. Your conception of Love didn't surprise me at all, though. In so far as I can judge by your words, c you saw Love as an object of love, rather than as a lover; that would explain why you imagined that Love was so attractive. I mean, it's true that a lovable object has to be blessed with beauty, charm, perfection and so on, but a lover comes from a different mould, whose characteristics I've described."

'"Well, Diotima," I remarked, "I like what you're saying, but if that's what Love is like, what do we humans gain from him?"

d '"That's the next point for me to try to explain, then, Socrates," she said. "I mean, we've covered Love's nature and parentage, but there's also the fact that, according to you, he loves beauty. Suppose we were to be asked, 'Can you two tell me in what sense Love loves attractive things?' or, more clearly, 'A lover loves attractive things—but why?'"

'"Because he wants them to be his," I suggested.

'"But your answer begs another question," she pointed out. "What will a person gain if he gets these attractive things?"

'I confessed that I didn't find that a particularly easy question to answer and she went on, 'Well, suppose the e questioner changed tack and phrased his question in terms of goodness instead of attractiveness. Suppose he asked, 'Now then, Socrates, a lover loves good things—but why?'"

'"He wants them to be his," I replied.

'"And what will a person gain if he gets these good things?"

'"That's a question I think I can cope with better," I said. "He'll be happy."

205a '"The point being that it's the possession of good things that makes people happy," she said, "and there's no need for a further question about a person's reasons for wanting to be happy. Your answer seems conclusive."*

'"That's right," I said.

'"Now, do you think this desire, this love, is common to all of us? Do you think everyone wants good things to be his for ever, or do you have a different view?"

'"No," I said. "I think it's common to everyone."

'"But if everyone loves the same thing, and always does so, Socrates," she said, "why don't we describe

everyone as a lover, instead of using the term selectively, b
for some people but not for others?"

' "Yes, that *is* odd, isn't it?" I said.

' "Not really," she replied. "What we do, in fact, is
single out a particular kind of love and apply to it the
term which properly belongs to the whole range. We call
it 'love' and use other terms for other kinds of love."

' "Can you give me an analogy?" I asked.

' "Yes, here's one. As you know, there are all kinds
of creativity. It's always creativity, after all, which is
responsible for something coming into existence when it
didn't exist before. And it follows that all artefacts are c
actually creations or poems and that all artisans are
creators or poets."*

' "Right."

' "As you also know, however," she went on, "artisans are referred to in all sorts of ways, not exclusively
as poets. Just one part of the whole range of creativity,
the part whose domain is music and metre, has been
singled out and has gained the name of the whole range.
The term 'poetry' is reserved for it alone, and it's only
those with creativity in this sense who are called 'poets'."

' "You're right," I said.

' "The same goes for love. Basically, it's always the d
case that the desire for good and for happiness is everyone's 'dominant, deceitful love'.* But there are a wide
variety of ways of expressing this love, and those who
follow other routes—for instance, business, sport, or
philosophy—aren't said to be in love or to be lovers.
The terminology which properly applies to the whole
range is used only of those who dedicate themselves to
one particular manifestation—which is called 'love' and
'being in love', while they're called 'lovers'."

' "I suppose you're right," I said.

' "Now," she continued, "what of the idea one hears
that people in love are looking for their other halves?*
What I'm suggesting, by contrast, my friend, is that love e
isn't a search for a half or even a whole unless the half or
the whole happens to be good. I mean, we're even

prepared to amputate our arms and legs if we think they're in a bad state. It's only when a person describes what he's got as good and what he hasn't got as bad that he's capable of being content with what belongs to him. In other words, the sole object of people's love is good-
206a ness. Do you agree?"

' "Definitely," I said.

' "So," she said, "the simple truth of the matter is that people love goodness. Yes?"

' "Yes," I answered.

' "But hadn't we better add that they want to *get* goodness for themselves?" she asked.

' "Yes."

' "And that's not all: there's also the fact that they want goodness to be theirs *for ever*," she said.

' "Yes, we'd better add that too."

' "To sum up, then," she said, "the object of love is the permanent possession of goodness for oneself."

' "You're absolutely right," I agreed.

b ' "Now since this is Love's purpose* in *all* his mani-festations," she said, "we need to ask under what conditions and in what sphere of activity the deter-mination and energy of people with this purpose may be called love.* What does love actually do? Can you tell me?"

' "Of course not, Diotima," I said. "If I could, I wouldn't be so impressed by your knowledge. This is exactly what I come to *you* to learn about."

' "All right," she said. "I'll tell you. Love's pur-pose is physical and mental procreation in an attractive medium."*

' "I don't understand what you mean," I said. "I need a diviner to interpret it for me."

c ' "All right," she said. "I'll speak more plainly. The point is, Socrates, that every human being is both phy-sically and mentally pregnant. Once we reach a certain point in the prime of our lives, we instinctively desire to give birth, but we find it possible only in an attractive medium, not a repulsive one—and yes, sex between a man and a woman is a kind of birth.* It's a divine business; it is immortality in a mortal creature, this matter of pregnancy and birth. But it can't take place where there's incompatibility, and whereas repulsiveness is incompatible with anything divine, beauty is compatible with it. So Beauty plays the parts of both Fate and Eileithyia at childbirth.* That's why proximity to beauty makes a pregnant person obliging, happy, and relaxed, and so we procreate and give birth. Proximity to repulsiveness, however, makes us frown, shrink in pain, back off, and withdraw; no birth takes place, but we retain our children unborn and suffer badly. So the reason why, when pregnant and swollen, ready to burst, we get so excited in the presence of beauty is that the bearer of beauty releases us from our agony. You see, Socrates," she concluded, "the object of love is not beauty, as you imagine."

'"What is it, then?"

'"It is birth and procreation in a beautiful medium."*

'"All right," I said.

'"It certainly is," she said. "Why procreation? Because procreation is as close as a mortal can get to being immortal and undying. Given our agreement that the aim of love is the *permanent* possession of goodness for oneself, it necessarily follows that we desire immortality along with goodness, and consequently the aim of love has to be immortality as well."*

'You can see how much I learned from what she said about the ways of love. Moreover, she once asked me, "Socrates, what do you think causes this love and desire? I mean, you can see what a terrible state animals of all kinds—beasts and birds—get into when they're seized by the desire for procreation. Their behaviour becomes manic under the influence of love. First, all they want is sex with one another, then all they want is to nurture their offspring. The weakest creatures are ready to fight even the strongest ones to the death and to sacrifice themselves for their young; they'll go to any lengths, including extreme starvation, if that's what it

takes to nurture their young. If it were only human beings," she pointed out, "you might think this behaviour was based on reason; but what causes animals to behave this way under the influence of love? Can you
c explain it?"

'When I said that I had no idea, she asked, "How do you expect to become an expert in the ways of love if you don't understand this?"

'"But that's exactly why I come to you, Diotima, as I've told you before, because I'm aware of my need for teachers. So will you explain it to me, please—and also anything else I need to know about the ways of love?"

'"Well," she said, "provided you're confident about the view we've expressed time and again about what love aims for, you shouldn't be surprised to hear that the same argument applies to animals as to humans: mortal
d nature does all it can to achieve immortality and live for ever. Its sole resource for this is the ability of reproduction constantly to replace the past generation with a new one. I mean, even during the period when any living creature is said to be a living creature and not to change . . . you know how we say that someone is the same person from childhood all the way up to old age. Although we say this, a person in fact never possesses the same attributes, but is constantly being renewed and constantly losing other qualities; this goes for his hair,
e flesh, bones, blood, and body in general. But it's not just restricted to the body: no one's mental characteristics, traits, beliefs, desires, delights, troubles, or fears ever remain the same: they come and go. But what is far more extraordinary even than this is the fact that our
208a knowledge comes and goes as well: we gain some pieces of information and lose others. The implication of this is not just that *we* don't remain the same for ever as far as our knowledge is concerned either, but that exactly the same thing happens to every single item of information. What we call 'practice', for instance, exists because knowledge leaks away. Forgetfulness is the leakage of information, and practice is the repeated renewal of

vanishing information in one's memory, which preserves the knowledge. This is what makes the knowledge *appear* to be the same as before.

'"The point is that the continued existence of any mortal creature does not involve its remaining absolutely unchanging for all time—only gods do that. Instead, as its attributes pass away and age, they leave behind a new b generation of attributes which resemble the old ones. This process is what enables mortal life—a body or whatever*—to share in immortality, Socrates, but immortal beings do things differently. So you shouldn't be surprised if everything instinctively values its own offspring: it is immortality which makes this devotion, which is love, a universal feature."

'In fact, I did find what she'd said surprising, so I said, "Well, you're the expert, Diotima, but is what you've been telling me really so?"

'She answered like a true sophist* and said, "You can c be sure of it, Socrates. I mean, you can see the same principle at work in men's lives too, if you take a look at their status-seeking. You'll be surprised at your stupidity if you fail to appreciate the point of what I've been saying once you've considered how horribly people behave when they're under the influence of love of prestige and they long to 'store up fame immortal for ever'.* Look how they're even more willing to face danger for the sake of fame than they are for their children; look how they spend money, endure any kind of hardship, d sacrifice their lives. Do you really think that Alcestis would have died for Admetus, that Achilles would have joined Patroclus in death,* or that your Athenian hero Codrus would have died in defence of his sons' kingdom, if they didn't think their courage would be remembered for ever, as in fact it is by us? No, they certainly wouldn't," she said. "I'm not sure that the prospect of undying virtue and fame of this kind isn't what motivates people to do anything, and that the better they are, the more this is their motivation. The point is, they're in e love with immortality.

51

'"Now, when men are *physically* pregnant," she continued, "they're more likely to be attracted to women; their love manifests in trying to gain immortality, renown, and what they take to be happiness by producing children. Those who are *mentally* pregnant, however . . . I

209a mean, there are people whose minds are far more pregnant than their bodies; they're filled with the offspring you might expect a mind to bear and produce. What offspring? Virtue, and especially wisdom. For instance, there are the creations brought into the world by the poets and any craftsmen who count as having done original work, and then there's the most important and attractive kind of wisdom by far, the kind which enables people to manage political and domestic affairs—in other words, self-discipline and justice. And here's another case: when someone's mind has been pregnant

b with virtue from an early age and he's never had a partner, then once he reaches adulthood, he longs to procreate and give birth, and so he's another one, in my opinion, who goes around searching for beauty, so that he can give birth there, since he'll never do it in an unattractive medium. Since he's pregnant, he prefers physical beauty to ugliness, and he's particularly pleased if he comes across a mind which is attractive, upright, and gifted at the same time. This is a person he immediately finds he can talk fluently to about virtue and about what qualities and practices it takes for a man to be

c good. In short, he takes on this person's education.*

'"What I'm saying, in other words, is that once he's come into contact with an attractive person and become intimate with him, he produces and gives birth to the offspring he's been pregnant with for so long. He thinks of his partner all the time, whether or not he's there, and together they share in raising their offspring. Consequently, this kind of relationship involves a far stronger bond and far more constant affection than is experienced by people who are united by ordinary children, because the offspring of this relationship are particularly attractive and are closer to immortality than ordinary children.* We'd all prefer to have children of this sort rather than the human kind, and we cast envious glances at good poets like Homer and Hesiod because the kind d of children they leave behind are those which earn their parents renown and 'fame immortal', since the children themselves are immortal. Or what about the children Lycurgus left in Sparta who maintain the integrity of Sparta and, it's hardly going too far to say, of Greece as a whole? Then there's Solon, whom you Athenians hold in high regard as the father of your constitution. All over the world, in fact, in Greece and abroad, various e men in various places have on a number of occasions engendered virtue in some form or other by creating works of beauty for public display. Quite a few of these men have even been awarded cults before now because of the immortality of their children, whereas no human child has ever yet earned his father a cult.

' "Now, it's not impossible, Socrates, that you too could be initiated into the ways of love I've spoken of so far. But I don't know whether you're ready for the final 210a grade of Watcher,* which is where even the mysteries I've spoken of lead if you go about them properly. All I can do", she said, "is tell you about them, which I'm perfectly willing to do; you must try to follow as best you can.

' "The proper way to go about this business", she said, "is for someone to start as a young man by focusing on physical beauty and initially—this depends on whether his guide* is giving him proper guidance— to love just one person's body and to give birth in that medium to beautiful reasoning. He should realize next that the beauty of any one body hardly differs from that b of any other body, and that if it's physical beauty he's after, it's very foolish of him not to regard the beauty of all bodies as absolutely identical. Once he's realized this and so become capable of loving every single beautiful body in the world, his obsession with just one body grows less intense and strikes him as ridiculous and petty. The next stage is for him to value mental beauty

so much more than physical beauty that even if someone is almost entirely lacking the bloom of youth, but still has an attractive mind, that's enough to kindle his love
c and affection, and that's all he needs to give birth to and enquire after the kinds of reasoning which help young men's moral progress. And this in turn leaves him no choice but to look at what makes people's activities and institutions attractive and to see that here too any form of beauty is much the same as any other, so that he comes to regard physical beauty as unimportant. Then, after activities, he must press on towards the things people know, until he can see the beauty there too. Now he has beauty before his eyes in abundance, no longer a
d single instance of it; now the slavish love of isolated cases of youthful beauty or human beauty of any kind is a thing of the past, as is his love of some single activity. No longer a paltry and small-minded slave, he faces instead the vast sea of beauty, and in gazing upon it his boundless love of knowledge becomes the medium in which he gives birth to plenty of beautiful, expansive reasoning and thinking, until he gains enough energy and bulk there to catch sight of a unique kind of knowledge whose natural object is the kind of beauty I will now describe.
e   ' "Try as hard as you can to pay attention now," she said, "because anyone who has been guided and trained in the ways of love up to this point, who has viewed things of beauty in the proper order and manner,* will now approach the culmination of love's ways and will suddenly catch sight of something of unbelievable beauty—something, Socrates, which in fact gives meaning to all his previous efforts. What he'll see is, in the
211a first place, eternal; it doesn't come to be or cease to be, and it doesn't increase or diminish. In the second place, it isn't attractive in one respect and repulsive in another, or attractive at one time but not at another, or attractive in one setting but repulsive in another, or attractive here and repulsive elsewhere, depending on how people find it. Then again, he won't perceive beauty as a face or

hands or any other physical feature, or as a piece of reasoning or knowledge, and he won't perceive it as being anywhere else either—in something like a creature or the earth or the heavens. No, he'll perceive it in itself and by itself, constant and eternal, and he'll see b that every other beautiful object somehow partakes of it, but in such a way that their coming to be and ceasing to be don't increase or diminish it at all, and it remains entirely unaffected.*

'"So the right kind of love for a boy* can help you ascend from the things of this world until you begin to catch sight of *that* beauty, and then you're almost within striking distance of the goal. The proper way to go about or be guided through the ways of love is to start c with beautiful things in this world and always make the beauty I've been talking about the reason for your ascent. You should use the things of this world as rungs in a ladder. You start by loving one attractive body and step up to two; from there you move on to physical beauty in general, from there to the beauty of people's activities, from there to the beauty of intellectual endeavours, and from there you ascend to that final intellectual endeavour,* which is no more and no less than the study of *that* beauty, so that* you finally recognize true beauty.

'"What else could make life worth living, my dear d Socrates," the woman from Mantinea said, "than seeing true beauty? If you ever do catch sight of it, gold and clothing and good-looking boys and youths will pale into insignificance beside it. At the moment, however, you get so excited by seeing an attractive boy that you want to keep him in your sight and by your side for ever, and you'd be ready—you're far from being the only one, of course—to go without food and drink, if that were possible, and to try to survive only on the sight and presence of your beloved. How do you think someone would react, then, to the sight of beauty itself, in its perfect, immaculate purity—not beauty tainted by e human flesh and colouring and all that mortal rubbish, but absolute beauty, divine and constant? Do you think someone with his gaze fixed there has a miserable life? 212a Is that what you think about someone who uses the appropriate faculty to see beauty and enjoy its presence? I mean, don't you appreciate that there's no other medium in which someone who uses the appropriate faculty to see beauty can give birth to true goodness instead of phantom goodness, because it is truth rather than illusion whose company he is in? And don't you realize that the gods smile on a person who bears and nurtures true goodness and that, to the extent that any human being does, it is he who has the potential for immortality?"*

b   'So there you are, Phaedrus—not forgetting the rest of you. That's what Diotima told me, and I believe her. As a believer, I try to win others as well round to the view that, in the business of acquiring immortality, it would be hard for human nature to find a better partner than Love. That's the basis of *my* claim that everyone should treat Love with reverence, and that's why I for one consider the ways of love to be very important. So I follow them exceptionally carefully myself and recommend others to do the same. It's also why, today and every day, I do all I can to praise Love's power and courage.

c   'That's my contribution, then, Phaedrus. You can think of it as a eulogy of Love if you want, or you can call it whatever you like. It's up to you.'

That was Socrates' speech. During the applause, Aristophanes was trying to get a word in, because at one point* Socrates had referred to his speech, when suddenly there was a loud knocking at the front door. It sounded like people from a street-party, and they could hear a pipe-girl's voice.* Agathon called over his slaves d and said, 'Go and see who it is. If it's one of my friends, invite him in, but otherwise tell them the party's over and we're off to bed.'

A short while later, they heard the sound of Alcibiades,

extremely drunk, in the courtyard. He was bellowing, 'Where's Agathon? Take me to Agathon.' In he came, supported by the pipe-girl and some of the other people who were with him. He stood at the door wearing a chaplet of leafy ivy entwined with violets, and with rib- e bons galore trailing over his head,* and said, 'Greetings, gentlemen. Will you let someone who's drunk—very drunk, actually—join your party? If not, we'll just put a chaplet on Agathon, which is why we came, and then we'll be on our way. I couldn't come yesterday, you see, but here I am now, and I've got these ribbons on my head so that I can take them off *my* head and put them on the cleverest and most attractive man in the world, along with a public announcement to that effect.* I suppose you'll laugh at me, because I'm drunk, but even if you do, it doesn't make any difference: *I* know perfectly well I'm right. Come on, hurry up and tell me. 213a Do you agree to my terms? Can I come in and join you for a drink or not?'

Everyone shouted out for him to come in and find a place on a couch, and Agathon called him over. So his friends brought him in. On the way, he started to untie the ribbons, with the intention of putting them on Agathon, and they fell over his eyes. So he didn't see Socrates, but sat next to Agathon, between him and Socrates, who'd moved over when he saw him coming. b As soon as he was seated, he embraced Agathon and put the chaplet on him.

Agathon told his slaves to undo Alcibiades' shoes, so that he could lie on the couch. 'There's room here for three,' he said.

'Fine,' said Alcibiades. 'But who's this third person? Who have we here at the party with us?' Even while speaking, he was turning around to look. As soon as he saw Socrates, he leapt up and said, 'God, what's this? Socrates? You've been lurking there waiting for me— and this isn't the first time: you're always suddenly c popping up where I least expect to find you. What are you doing here this time? And why here, on this couch? I know: you didn't want to be next to Aristophanes and his jokes, or anyone else who might fancy himself a comedian, so you found a way to share a couch with the handsomest man at the party.'

'I need your protection, Agathon, please,' said Socrates. 'You can't imagine what a nuisance my love for this man has become. Ever since the start of our affair, I've d never been able to look at or talk to anyone attractive without him getting so jealous and resentful that he goes crazy and calls me names and comes close to beating me up. So please make sure that he doesn't get up to anything tonight. Perhaps you can calm things down between us, but if not, and if he starts to get violent, please protect me from him, because he gets insanely attached to his lovers, and it terrifies me.'

'There's no chance of peace between us,' Alcibiades said. 'Anyway, I'll pay *you* back later for what you've e been saying, but for now can you give me back some of the ribbons, please, Agathon, so that I can make a chaplet for his head too? And what a wonderful head! Otherwise, he'll tell me off for making one for you, but not for him, despite the fact that he beats all comers every day in battles of words, not just yesterday like you.'*

With these words, he took back some of the ribbons and made a chaplet for Socrates. Then he lay down on the couch, and once he'd settled down, he said, 'Well now, gentlemen, you look sober to me, and that's not allowed. You have to drink, because that was part of our agreement. We need somebody to take charge of your drinking* and decide when you've had enough, and I elect—me! Have a big goblet* brought in, won't you, Agathon, if you've got one? Oh no, don't bother. Hey you, slave, bring over that cooler.'*

He'd spotted a cooler with a capacity of more than 214a eight *kotylai*, and once it had been filled up, he first drained it himself and then told the slave to fill it for Socrates, while commenting, 'Not that this ploy of mine will do any good as far as Socrates is concerned. It

58

doesn't matter how much you tell him to drink, he drinks it all down without ever getting drunk.'

When the slave had filled it up, and while Socrates was drinking, Eryximachus said, 'What's going on here, Alcibiades? Are we just going to gulp drinks down like this, as if we had thirsts to quench? We could at b least make conversation or sing some songs as we drink.'

'Hello there, Eryximachus,' said Alcibiades, 'most noble son of a noble—and temperate—sire.'

'And hello to you too,' Eryximachus replied. 'But what would you have us do?'

'Whatever you suggest,' said Alcibiades. 'We ought to do as you say, "for a healer's worth is that of many men".* So we're yours to command.'

'All right,' said Eryximachus. 'Here's what I suggest. Before you arrived, we'd decided that each of us should take turns, going around from left to right, to speak as c well as he could in praise of Love. Now, all the rest of us have already spoken, so it's only fair, since you haven't had a turn (except at drinking), that you should deliver a speech. Then, when you've finished, you can choose a task to set Socrates, then he can do the same for the person on his right, and so on.'

'What a good idea, Eryximachus!' Alcibiades said. 'But I don't think it's fair to pit someone who's drunk against speeches delivered by sober men. Also, you don't believe a word of what Socrates was saying a moment ago, do you? I mean, the truth is exactly the opposite of d what he said, you know. It's *he* who'll beat me up if I praise anyone except him—even a god, let alone another human being—when he's around.'

'Be careful what you say,' Socrates said.

'No, I won't have you trying to talk me out of it,' said Alcibiades. 'I swear I'm not going to deliver a eulogy to anyone else while you're around.'

'All right, then,' Eryximachus said. 'Go ahead, if you want. Let's hear your eulogy of Socrates!'

'What?' Alcibiades exclaimed. 'Do you think I should, e

Eryximachus? Shall I lay into him and pay him back in front of all of you?'

'Hang on,' Socrates said. 'What are you planning to do—deliver a kind of mock eulogy of me, or what?'

'I'll tell the truth—if you'll let me do that.'

'Of course I'll let you tell the truth,' Socrates said. 'In fact, I insist that you do.'

'Here I go, then,' said Alcibiades. 'I'll tell you what you can do, Socrates. If anything I say isn't true, you can interrupt, if you want, and show that what I'm saying is wrong. Not that I intend any of what I'm going to say to
215a be untrue. But don't be surprised if I don't remember things in the right order: it isn't easy for someone in my condition to list all the aspects of your extraordinary nature and fluently tick them off, one after another.

'I'm going to use some imagery to help me praise Socrates, gentlemen. *He* might think I'm going for comic effect,* but actually the point of the imagery will be the truth, not mockery. It's my considered opinion, you see, that he's just like those Sileni you find sitting in
b sculptors' shops, the ones they make holding wind-pipes or reed-pipes, which when opened up are found to contain effigies of gods inside. Alternatively, I could compare him to Marsyas, the Satyr. Now, even you can't deny that you *look* like these figures,* Socrates, but what you're about to hear is how you resemble them in other respects as well.

'You treat people brutally*—now, don't try to deny it. If you do, I'll call up witnesses. But you don't play the pipes? No, because you're far more extraordinary than
c Marsyas. He had to use an instrument to charm people with his oral abilities, and even now anyone who plays his pipes—I'm counting Olympus' pipe-playing as really attributable to Marsyas, because Marsyas was Olympus' teacher* . . . Anyway, whether his pipes are played by an expert player or a worthless pipe-girl, there's no other instrument which is so divine that it's capable of casting a spell over people and of showing who is reaching for

the gods and is ready for initiation.* The only difference
between you and Marsyas is that *you* don't need any
instrument: you produce the same effect with plain
words! What I mean is this. If we're listening to even a d
first-rate speech from someone else, it's hardly an exaggeration to say that none of us takes the slightest bit of
notice of him; but when we hear you speaking, or listen
to even a second-rate report of one of your arguments,
then it doesn't matter who we are—woman, man or
child—we're all overwhelmed and spellbound.

'If it weren't for the fact that you would put it down
to the drink, gentlemen, I'd call on the gods to witness
the truth of my account of what I personally have
experienced when listening to him speak in the past—
which is not to say that he doesn't still have the same
effect on me even now. Whenever I listen to him speak, e
I get more ecstatic than the Corybantes!* My heart
pounds and tears flood from my eyes under the spell of
his words. I've seen him have the same effect on plenty
of others too. I've heard some great speakers, including
Pericles, and while I thought they did a good job, they
never had that kind of effect on me, and they never
disturbed my mental composure or made me dissatisfied
with the slavishness of my life. This Marsyas here,
however, has often changed my outlook and made me
think that the life I lead isn't worth living. You can't 216a
deny the truth of this, Socrates. In fact, I know perfectly
well that if I allowed myself to listen to him, I wouldn't
be able to resist even now, and I'd go through it all over
again. You see, he forces me to admit that I busy myself
with Athenian politics when I'm far from perfect and
should be doing something about myself instead. So I
make myself block my ears and run away, as if I were
escaping the Sirens; otherwise I'd spend the rest of my
life sitting there at his feet.

'He's the only person in the world in whose company
I've felt something which people wouldn't think I was b
capable of feeling—shame: I feel shame before him and
him alone. What happens is that although I'm perfectly

well aware of the inescapable force of his recommendations as to what I should do, yet as soon as I'm away from him, I get seduced by the adulation of the masses. So I act like a runaway slave and keep away from him, and whenever I do see him, I feel ashamed because of the promises I made him. In fact, there've been quite a few occasions when I'd gladly have seen him removed from c the face of the earth, but I also know that my predominant reaction by far to that happening would be sadness,* and so I just don't know how to cope with the man.

'So that's the kind of effect this Satyr here has on me, and on lots of other people too, with his piping. But I haven't finished with the ways in which he resembles the figures I compared him to, and I can give you further examples of his incredible abilities. You have to appreciate that none of you really knows him. Now that I've d started, I'll show you what he's like. The Socrates of your experience has a habit of falling in love with good-looking people, and he's constantly hanging around them in a stupor; secondly, he's completely ignorant and has no knowledge at all. Do you see how Silenus-like he looks?* The resemblance is striking. The point is, this is just an outer coating, like the outside shell of those carved Sileni. But if he were opened up, my friends, you'd find him chock-full of self-control inside. I tell you, the fact that someone is attractive doesn't matter to him at all; he has an unbelievably low opinion of that, e and the same goes for wealth and any of the other advantages which are commonly regarded as enviable. None of these possessions have the slightest value, according to him, and we amount to nothing. You must appreciate that he spends his whole life pretending and playing with people.

'I don't know if any of you has seen the genuine Socrates, opened up to reveal the effigies he has inside, but I saw them once, and they struck me as so divine, so 217a glorious, so gorgeous and wonderful that—to cut a long story short—I felt I should obey him in everything.

I thought he'd genuinely fallen for my charms and that this was a godsend, an amazing piece of good luck, because now, as his boyfriend, I'd be in a position to hear everything he knew. I was incredibly proud of my good looks, you see. Now, I'd never been alone with him: there was usually a slave in attendance as well. But once I'd got this idea in my mind, I dismissed the attendant and there I was, alone with him—yes, I know, b but I'm committed to telling you the whole truth, so please just listen. And Socrates, you're welcome to point out any time I stray from the truth.

'Anyway, there we were, gentlemen, the two of us together on our own. I thought he'd launch straight into the kind of conversation lovers make when they've got their boyfriends on their own, and this made me happy. But nothing like that happened at all. He talked to me in the way he always had, and at the end of the day off he went. Next, I invited him to join me in the gymnasium and we exercised together—I thought *that* would get c me somewhere!* Anyway, we exercised together and wrestled together, often with no one else around . . . and do I have to spell it out? I got precisely nowhere.

'Since these tactics weren't advancing my cause at all, I decided on a direct assault, and I determined to persevere with what I'd started and to find out what was going on. So I invited him to have dinner with me—for all the world as if I were the lover and he were the boy I had designs on. He didn't rush to accept this invitation either, but he did eventually say he'd come. The first d time he came, he wanted to leave after the meal, and I let him on that occasion because I was feeling ashamed of myself. But I continued with my plan, and the next time I kept him talking far into the night after we'd finished eating, and when he felt it was time to go, I pointed out how late it was and made him stay. So he settled down to sleep on the same couch he'd used at dinner, which was next to mine. And we were the only people sleeping in the house.

'Now, it would have been all right for anyone to have e

heard everything I've told you so far, but from now on you'll hear things I wouldn't have told you except that, firstly, truth comes from wine (as the saying goes), whether or not I take the slaves into consideration,* and secondly, I think it would be wrong of me to pass over Socrates' awe-inspiring behaviour when I'm supposed to be delivering a eulogy of him. Besides, I feel rather like someone who's been bitten by a snake, in the sense that people who've had this experience are, I'm told, reluctant to talk about what it was like except to someone who has also been bitten, on the grounds that he's the only one who'll know what they went through and will
218a make allowances for any shocking actions or remarks of theirs, as having been prompted by the pain. In fact, I've been bitten by something with a far more excruciating bite than a snake, and it couldn't have attacked a more vulnerable part of me. My heart or mind—I don't know what the proper term is—has been struck and bitten by philosophy, and when philosophy seizes on the mind of a young man of calibre, it clings more fiercely than any snake and makes him do and say all sorts of things. Besides, when I look around at people like Phaedrus,
b Agathon, Eryximachus, Pausanias, Aristodemus, and Aristophanes—and then there's Socrates himself and all the rest of you ... You've *all* experienced the madness and ecstasy of philosophy, and that's why I can talk in front of you, because you'll make allowances for what I did then and what I'm going to say now. But you slaves had better batten sizeable hatches down on your ears, and the same goes for any other coarse non-initiates here.*

'So anyway, gentlemen, when the lamp had been
c extinguished and the slaves had left the room, I decided to cut out the frills and come right out with my thoughts. I nudged him and said, "Socrates, are you asleep?"

'"No, far from it," he answered.

'"Do you know what I've been thinking?"

'"What's that, then?"

'"I think you're in love with me," I said, "and that

you're the only lover I've got who's good enough for me. You're too shy to bring it up in my company, so I'll tell you what *I* feel. I think it would be stupid of me not to gratify you in this and in anything else you want*—anything that is mine to give or that I can get from my friends. You see, there's nothing more important to me than becoming as good a person as I can, and I think no one offers more effective assistance in this than you. I'd be far more ashamed, then, of what people of intelligence would think of me if I didn't gratify someone who has so much to offer than of what the ignorant masses would think of me if I did." d

'His response to my words was absolutely typical—full of mock modesty, as you'd expect. "My dear Alcibiades," he said, "it looks as though you really are no ordinary person. Suppose your opinion of me is actually true and I do somehow have the ability to make you a e better person. You must find me remarkably attractive, then, with a beauty that is infinitely superior to your own good looks. Now, if this is what you see in me, and you then try to make a deal with me which involves us trading our respective beauties, then you're planning to do quite a bit better than me out of it; you're trying to give the semblance of beauty and get truth in return. In other words, this is a real 'gold for bronze'* exchange 219a you're planning. But anyway, I think you'd better have a closer look, otherwise you might make the mistake of thinking I've got something to offer. I tell you, it's only when your eyesight goes into decline* that your mental vision begins to see clearly, and you've got a long way to go yet."

' "As far as I'm concerned," I replied, "my plans are no more and no less than what I've said. That leaves it up to you to decide what's best, in your opinion, for you and for me."

' "Now, *that* is a good idea," he said. "Yes, from now on we'll put our heads together and do whatever seems best. This goes for everything, not just the issue currently b facing us."

'After this conversation, I thought the shots I'd fired, so to speak, had wounded him, so I got up from my couch, and before he had time to say anything else, I put my thick cloak over him (it was winter) and lay down under his short cloak.* I put my arms around this

c remarkable, wonderful man—he is, you know—and lay there with him all night long. No, you can't deny the truth of this either, Socrates. And after all that, he spurned and disdained and scorned my charms so thoroughly, and treated me so brutally—and remember, gentlemen of the jury, this was something I prided myself on* . . . I might as well call you "gentlemen of the jury", because you're listening to evidence of Socrates' high-handed treatment of me. Anyway, the point is— and I call on all the gods and goddesses in heaven to witness the truth of this—that I got up the next morning, after having spent the night with Socrates, and

d for all the naughtiness we'd got up to, I might as well have been sleeping with my father or an elder brother.

'What do you think my state of mind was after that? Although I felt I'd been insulted, I was full of admiration for his character, self-control, and courage. I'd never have believed such a man could exist—that I could come across such intelligence and resolve. So although I couldn't possibly feel cross with him and keep away from him, I couldn't find a way to make him mine

e either. I mean, I was well aware that you'd be more likely to get a weapon through Ajax's guard than you would money through Socrates', and now he'd escaped the only trap I thought stood a chance of ensnaring him. So I didn't know what to do, and there I was: no slave has ever been more utterly in the power of any master than I was in his.

'This was the situation I was already in when we saw active service together at Potidaea* and shared a mess there. Now, the first thing to point out is that there was no one better than him in the whole army at enduring hardship: it wasn't just me he showed up. Once, when we were cut off (as happens during a campaign), we had

to do without food and no one else could cope at all. At 220a
the same time, when there *were* plenty of provisions, he
was better than the rest of us at making the most of
them, and especially when it came to drinking: he was
reluctant to drink, but when pushed he proved more
than a match for everyone. And the most remarkable thing of all is that no one has ever seen Socrates
drunk.*

'Anyway, I expect he'll be tested on this point a
little later tonight. Meanwhile, back to Potidaea, where
the winters are terrible, but Socrates' endurance of
them was miraculous. Once—and this was the most
astonishing thing he did—the cold was so terribly bitter b
that everyone was either staying inside or, if they did
venture out, they wore an incredible amount of clothing,
put shoes on, and then wrapped pieces of felt and
sheepskin around their feet. Socrates, however, went out
in this weather wearing only the outdoor cloak he'd
usually worn earlier in the campaign as well, and without anything on his feet; but he still made his way
through the ice more easily than the rest of us with our
covered feet. His fellow soldiers thought he was setting
himself up as superior to them, and they gave him
suspicious looks.   c

'So much for that episode, "but here's another exploit
the indomitable man performed"* once during the campaign there, and it's well worth hearing. One morning,
a puzzling problem occurred to him and he stayed
standing where he was thinking about it. Even when it
proved intractable, he didn't give up: he just stood there
exploring it. By the time it was midday, people were
beginning to notice him and were telling one another in
amazement that Socrates had been standing there from
early in the morning deep in thought. Eventually, after
their evening meal, some men from the Ionian con-
tingent took their pallets outside—it was summer at the d
time—so that they could simultaneously sleep outside
where it was cool and watch out for whether he'd stand
there all night as well. In fact, he stood there until after

sunrise the following morning, and then he greeted the sun with a prayer and went on his way.

'Then there's his behaviour in combat; I owe him an account of this, to cover my debt. You see, during the battle which led to my being awarded the prize for valour by the commanding officers, my life was saved by one man and one man alone—Socrates. He refused to
e leave me when I was wounded, and he kept my weapons and armour safe, as well as my life.* I *told* the commanding officers at the time that it was you who should be awarded the prize for valour,* Socrates: you won't find anything to tell me off for here, or any reason to claim I'm lying either. But the commanding officers had an eye on my status and wanted to award it to me, and you were actually more insistent than them that it should go to me rather than you.

'And that's not all, gentlemen. You should have seen Socrates during the army's hasty withdrawal from
221a Delium.* I was serving in the cavalry there, in fact, while Socrates was a hoplite.* The army had scattered into small units, and I happened to come across Socrates trying to make his way back with Laches. As soon as I saw them, I told them not to lose heart and promised to stay with them. Now, I was even better placed to observe Socrates there than I was at Potidaea, because being on horseback I didn't have to worry so much for my own safety. The main thing I noticed was how much more self-possessed he was than Laches; secondly, it struck me how even in that situation he was walking
b along just as he does here in Athens—as you put it, Aristophanes, "with head held high and eyes alert",* calmly looking out for friends and enemies. Anyone could tell, even from a distance, that here was a man who would resist an attack with considerable determination. And that's why he and Laches got out of there safely, because the enemy generally don't take on someone who can remain calm during combat; they prefer to
c go after people who are in headlong flight.

'There are many other remarkable things about Socrates which could feature in a eulogy, but most of the things he does could perhaps be paralleled in some other person's life. However, what's absolutely astonishing about the man is his uniqueness: there's no human being, from times past or present, who can match him. For example, you can compare Achilles to Brasidas and others, or Pericles to Nestor and Antenor (to name only two), and you can find the same kinds of correspon- d dences for other people. But this man here is so out of the ordinary that however hard you look you'll never find anyone from any period who remotely resembles him, and the way he speaks is just as unique as well. All you can do, in fact, is what I did, and compare him and his arguments not to any human being, but to Sileni and Satyrs.

'The point is, you see, that I forgot to mention at the beginning that his conversations too are just like those Sileni you can open up. The first time a person lets himself listen to one of Socrates' arguments, it sounds e really ridiculous. Trivial-sounding words and phrases form his arguments' outer coating, the brutal Satyr's skin.* He talks of pack-asses, metal-workers, shoe-makers, tanners;* he seems to go on and on using the same arguments to make the same points, with the result that ignoramuses and fools are bound to find his argu-ments ridiculous. But if you could see them opened up, if 222a you can get through to what's under the surface, what you'll find inside is that his arguments are the only ones in the world which make sense. And that's not all: under the surface, his arguments abound with divinity and effigies of goodness. They turn out to be extremely far-reaching, or rather they cover absolutely everything which needs to be taken into consideration on the path to true goodness.

'That's what I have to say in praise of Socrates, gentlemen—though I've included some critical com-ments as well, and told you how brutally he treated me. I'm not the only one, in fact, to have received this treat-ment from him: there's Charmides the son of Glaucon, b

Euthydemus the son of Diocles, and a great many others too. He takes people in by pretending to be their lover, and then he swaps roles and becomes their beloved instead. So I'm warning you, Agathon: don't be duped by him like this. Learn from *our* experiences and take care. You don't have to behave like the proverbial fool and experience something yourself before understanding it.'*

c So that was Alcibiades' speech. People found his candour amusing, because he was evidently still in love with Socrates. And Socrates said, 'It's you who are sober, I think,* Alcibiades. Otherwise, the elegance with which you surrounded and tried to conceal the underlying motive of your whole speech would have been beyond you. You just added it on at the end, as if it were an aside—as if the whole point of your speech hadn't been
d to make me and Agathon fall out with each other, because you think that I ought to love you and nobody else, and Agathon ought to be loved by you and nobody else. Well, you didn't get away with it: we saw through this Satyrical, Silenus-like play-acting of yours.* My dear Agathon, he mustn't succeed: please make sure that no one comes between us.'

'I think you're probably right, Socrates,' Agathon
e replied. 'Did you notice how he lay down on the couch with you and me to either side of him? He *has* come between us, literally! But that's the limit of his success: I'll come and lie next to you.'

'Please do,' said Socrates. 'Lie down here on the other side of me.'

'Oh God!' groaned Alcibiades. 'Look at what he puts me through! He thinks he always has to go one better than me. Come on, Socrates, you could at least let Agathon lie between us.'*

'No, that's not on,' Socrates replied. 'I mean, *you*'ve delivered a eulogy of *me*, and now *I* have to deliver a eulogy of the person on my right.* If Agathon moves between us, then surely he'll have to eulogize me all over

again, won't he, before I've had time to eulogize him
instead? No, forget it, Alcibiades. Don't deprive him of 223a
the chance of having me sing his praises; I'm really
looking forward to doing it.'

'Oh!' cried Agathon. 'Alcibiades, I can't possibly stay
here! I really must change places, so that I can be the
subject of a eulogy from Socrates!'

'This is typical,' said Alcibiades. 'When Socrates is
around, nobody else gets a look-in at any attractive
man. Do you see how glibly he's found a plausible
reason why this handsome man should lie down next to
him?'

Agathon had stood up to go and lie next to Socrates, b
when a large number of people from a street-party
suddenly arrived at the front door. They found it open,
because someone was just leaving, so they barged straight
in to where the others were and settled themselves down
on couches. Everything went utterly out of control; all
there was left to do was to drink a great deal, and even
that was completely unsystematic.*

Aristodemus said that a few people, including Eryximachus and Phaedrus, left at this point, while he fell
asleep and slept for a long time, since the nights were c
long. When he woke up, it was almost light and cocks
were already crowing. Once his eyes were open, he
could see that although by and large people were asleep
or had gone home, Agathon, Aristophanes, and Socrates
were still awake, all by themselves, and were drinking
from a large bowl which they were passing round from
left to right. Socrates was carrying on a conversation
with them. Aristodemus said he couldn't remember
most of the discussion, because he'd missed the start of d
it and anyway he was sleepy, but the nub of it, he said,
was that Socrates was trying to get them to agree that
knowing how to compose comedies and knowing how
to compose tragedies must combine in a single person
and that a professional tragic playwright was also
a professional comic playwright.* They were coming
round to his point of view, but they were too sleepy to

follow the argument very well; Aristophanes fell asleep first and Agathon joined him after daybreak.

Now that he'd put them to sleep, Socrates got up and left. Aristodemus went with him, as usual. Socrates went to the Lyceum* for a wash, spent the day as he would any other, and then went home to sleep in the evening.

EXPLANATORY NOTES

172a *what you're asking about*: Apollodorus addresses the whole dialogue to a group of unnamed companions, only one of whom speaks. This is the second time in two days that Apollodorus tells the story (the previous time to someone called Glaucon). Nussbaum's fanciful theory that these two narrations bracket the news of Alcibiades' death reaching Athens is so brilliant that it scarcely matters whether or not it is right.

172a *Phalerum*: a village on the coast south-west of Athens.

172a *a bit of fun*: it is not perfectly clear what is amusing about what he says. Textual emendation has been suggested, but short of that, we are probably to imagine a bantering tone of voice.

173a *victory rites*: the date is 416 BC. The best few plays written each year in Athens were financed by wealthy citizens (as a form of tax) and entered into a competition during a festival of Dionysus. Unless later generations thought the plays absolutely exceptional, this would be their sole public performance.

173b *never wears shoes*: for administrative purposes, Athenian citizens belonged to 'demes', which were districts of Attica. Xenophon (*Memoirs of Socrates* 1. 4) also remarks on Aristodemus' lack of height; in not wearing shoes, he imitated Socrates.

173b *lovers*: for Socrates' pupils as his lovers, see pp. xvii–xviii.

173d *the softy*: there is in fact a strongly attested textual variant which would entail the translation, 'I've no idea how you came to get your nickname "the fanatic", but it's true that your conversational tone...' But the version I have translated is slightly more natural Greek, and may be argued to make sense in the light of what little we know of Apollodorus from elsewhere: that he was notoriously homosexual, and wept copiously at Socrates' death (Plato, *Phaedo* 117d). Those who are interested in arguments for and against either reading can consult the sequence of articles by J. D. Moore, G. J. de Vries, and J. B. Skemp in *Mnemosyne*, 22 and 23 (1969 and 1970).

174a *bathed and wearing shoes!*: for Socrates' shoelessness, see 220b and note on 173b. If it was unusual for Socrates to have bathed, this does not necessarily mean he neglected personal hygiene more than his peers. After exercising, an Athenian

73

might have his body oiled and then all the sweat and dirt scraped off with a strigil, and once in a while he might take a full bath; but bathing only became a common occurrence in the Western world in the last hundred years or so.

174b *good men's feasts*: retaining ἀγαθῶν with the MSS. Evidently, the proverb Plato is thinking of is the ᴏne preserved in fragment 289 Kock of the comic poet Eupolis: 'Good men go of their own accord to bad men's feasts.' The alteration allows him to produce an untranslatable pun: the italicized 'distortion' is almost identical in form to Agathon's name.

174c *feeble fighter*: Homer, *Iliad* 17. 588. Menelaus arrives at his brother's celebration at 2. 408.

174d *up the road*: a deliberate misquote of part of Homer, *Iliad* 10. 224.

175a *Eryximachus' couch*: two to a couch was perfectly normal: this does not mean that Aristodemus' presence is any inconvenience. When Socrates arrives, he will double up on Agathon's couch, and later Alcibiades will make it three there.

175a *on the couch*: his feet were cleaned so as not to dirty the couch (remember that Greeks wore sandals, and the roads were dusty); and his hands were cleaned for eating.

175c *end couch to himself*: see p. xiv for the room's arrangement.

175e *to witness it*: Socrates is exaggerating for mock flattery, but not as much as it might seem to a modern reader: in Athens, plays were performed on public holidays, and the theatre could accommodate about ten thousand people. The number 'thirty thousand' meant 'countless' or 'a very large number'.

175e *arbiter*: because they will be drinking, and Dionysus is the god of wine. But Agathon may also be expressing confidence in the ultimate decision, since his tragedy has just won first prize in the Lenaea, a festival sacred to Dionysus. However, when it comes to a debate between the two of them, Agathon confesses himself beaten (201c); and at 213e Socrates' superiority in this respect to Agathon is confirmed by Alcibiades, who personifies Dionysus (see notes on 212e and 220a).

176e *external compulsion*: normally, a 'president' would decide how often guests' goblets were refilled, and how diluted the wine would be with water. His decisions were final. This explains why in the preceding conversation they have anticipated (with dread) having to drink a certain amount of wine.

In the present party, this presidential function has been decided on democratically—until Alcibiades' arrival (213e).

176e *women in their quarters*: it would be unusual for respectable women to be present at a symposium. It was not uncommon for the female entertainers at a party (like the pipe-girl here) to become sexual partners later in the evening. The girl's instrument was the *aulos* or reed-pipe; players often played a pair of pipes at once, with the melody being played on one while the other droned.

177a *Phaedrus here*: a parody of a line from Euripides' lost *Melanippe*—'The tale is not mine, but comes from my mother' (fragment 488. 1 Nauck²).

177b *encomium to him*: this might strike us as surprising, heirs as we are of the great traditions of Arabic love-poetry, Courtly Love, and Romanticism; but it is true that in Greek culture Love was not treated as a major deity and that the poets had generally deplored his effects rather than sung his praises.

177b *for instance*: a summary of Prodicus' 'Choice of Heracles' is preserved in Xenophon, *Memorabilia* 2. 1. 21–34. It tells how Heracles chose the rough road of virtue over the easy path of vice. The term 'sophist' originally meant 'clever professional teacher', rather than 'casuist'.

177b *a clever author*: possibly the Athenian sophist Polycrates, who is best known for his posthumous assault on Socrates, which is reflected in the opening chapters of Xenophon's *Memorabilia*.

177d *all I understand*: see note on 204a, and pp. xvi–xviii.

177e *won't object*: since they are in love with each other: see note on 181d.

177e *ever occupied with*: as a comic playwright in the ribald mode of Old Comedy, wine (Dionysus) and sex (Aphrodite) featured prominently in Aristophanes' work.

178b *Hesiod*: Hesiod's authority in the field of divine genealogy was paramount, thanks to his *Theogony*. Plato has Phaedrus quote lines 116–17 and the beginning of line 120 (lines 118–19 may be a later interpolation). 'Chaos' is a transliteration: the word means a kind of primal lack of differentiation of anything. Phaedrus' citations are rather partisan, though, since other poets ascribed parentage to Love.

178b *was Love*: Parmenides, fragment 13 Diels–Kranz. 'She' is the goddess who occupies the centre of the universe, who may be

the Lady Necessity. At 178b8–c1 I read (following Renehan)
Ἡσιόδῳ δὲ καὶ Ἀκουσίλεως ὁμολογεῖ. Παρμενίδης . . .

178c *virtuous lover*: the reader will soon see that in Athenian society
'lover' (*erastēs*) did not mean just 'someone involved in a love
affair', as it does in English, but was a technical term, within a
homosexual relationship, for the dominant partner, who was
assumed to be older and to pursue the teenager or young man,
for whom passive terms such as 'loved one' or 'beloved'
(*erōmenos*) and 'boyfriend' (*paidika*) are used.

178e *and their boyfriends*: omitting ἤ in e5 (Rückert).

179a *conquer the whole world*: as a matter of fact, the Thebans did
create a homosexual battalion, called the Sacred Band, in 378
BC. Since Plato's Phaedrus seems to be unaware of the actual
existence of such a battalion, this allows us to date the composition of *Symposium* between 385 (see note on 193a) and
378.

179b *some hero or other*: for instance, Diomedes at *Iliad* 10. 482.

179e *Isles of the Blessed*: a part of the underworld traditionally
reserved for the élite (by whatever standards different sources
judge élitism) after their death.

179e *his lover Patroclus*: actually, Homer nowhere explicitly portrays the two friends as homosexual lovers. It was not unknown
in ancient times to portray them as such, but the issue is still
debated by scholars. The famous choice of Achilles—a long,
inglorious life or a short, illustrious one—can be found in
Homer's *Iliad*, 9. 410–16.

180a *he claims*: in the lost play *Myrmidons*.

180a *as Homer records*: *Iliad* 11. 786 has Patroclus the older of the
two, but Homer does not say that he is *much* older.

180e *called Common*: note that the word translated 'Celestial'
(*Uranios*) is cognate with Uranus, whose name means 'the
heavens'. Aphrodite was in fact worshipped under both these
titles. Pausanias' account of the different parentage of the two
Aphrodites is a reflection of two different sources: in Homer,
Iliad 5. 370 ff., Aphrodite is the daughter of Zeus and Dione;
in Hesiod, *Theogony* 190 ff., we get the story of Aphrodite's
birth from the foam (*aphros*) caused by Uranus' castrated
genitals splashing into the sea. Common Aphrodite is called
younger than Celestial Aphrodite simply because of the stan-

dard genealogy of the gods: Uranus was Zeus' grandfather, so Celestial Aphrodite is the great-aunt of Common Aphrodite!

181a *deserves our praise*: notice the rather blatant contradiction with the pious sentiment with which the paragraph opened.

181b *the most unintelligent people imaginable*: that is, women, who were regarded in Greek patriarchal culture as inherently irrational, like pre-pubertal children (181d) and animals. Despite this prevailing view, Pausanias the champion of homosexuality is stating his case rather strongly.

181c *no trace of femininity*: because she has no mother.

181c *treating people brutally*: since ancient Greek society was more tolerant of a wider variety of sexual behaviour than modern Western societies, it tended to distinguish between acceptable and non-acceptable forms of behaviour as much as anything by the absence or presence of 'brutality' (*hubris*). One thinker, contemporary with Socrates, even defined 'legitimate love' as 'the pursuit of beauty without *hubris*' (Democritus, fragment 73 Diels–Kranz). However, what counted as *hubris* was also socially determined: the Greek male attitude towards the traditionally passive partners in a sexual relationship—women, boys, and slaves—would be *hubris* by most people's standards today.

181d *running off to someone else*: we should imagine Pausanias gazing fondly at Agathon during this paragraph. One of the few biographical facts we know about him is that his affair with Agathon had already been going on for about a dozen years by the time of this symposium, and that when Agathon left Athens for Macedonia ten years later, Pausanias went with him. Their relationship was the perfect example of a lifelong homosexual love-affair.

182a *inopportune and immoral behaviour*: because they have affairs with boys who are too young, and then do them wrong by abandoning them.

182a *in Sparta*: Plato does not talk about Spartan customs here, but to judge by Xenophon, *Constitution of Sparta* 2. 12–14, they too differentiated between homosexual love where the object was the moral improvement of the younger partner, and that where the object was sexual satisfaction.

182b *the Persian empire*: the Greek cities of Ionia (along the central part of the western coast of Asia Minor) were from time to time subject to Persian influence or even domination. However, Plato is being anachronistic. At the dramatic date of *Symposium* (416), the cities were in fact under Athenian influence; at the time Plato was writing, however (*c*.380—see note on 179a), Persia was dominant.

182c *downfall of the tyrants*: see the Index of Names, under Harmodius, for the story.

183a *unmitigated disapproval*: I exclude φιλοσοφίας as a gloss, with Schleiermacher and recent editors. Dover's careful analyses (1964 and 1978) suggest that Pausanias is exaggerating if he means to give the impression that Athenian society as a whole encouraged homosexuality. It condoned it, but it was only actually encouraged in the upper-class circles in which Plato's characters moved. Pausanias' description of Athenian ambivalence, then, is a fiction designed to support his division of Love into good and bad.

183d *gratification of a good man*: in what follows, Pausanias does not contrast mere physical lust with a relationship which transcends sex, as Diotima will later, but with a full relationship including physical sex as well as affection and instruction.

183e *and is gone*: a snatch from Homer, *Iliad* 2. 71, on the evanescence of a dream.

184c *by increasing one's knowledge*: as a master does for an apprentice: this was a perfectly acceptable form of service, of course.

184e *increase his knowledge*: omitting εἰς (Schütz).

185c *rhetorical balancing*: not just in the 'balance' (as the Greeks called it) of the pun between 'Pausanias' and 'pause', but in the balanced length and rhythm of 'Once Pausanias' and 'had come to a pause'.

185d *get rid of my hiccups*: not just because he is a doctor, but because his name could be translated 'one who fights belches'.

186c *bodily filling and emptying*: the principle of balance was crucial to ancient Greek medicine. If a body was too 'full' in some respect, it had to be emptied, while if it was too 'empty', it had to be filled; if there was too much of one element (heat, for instance), that fullness would have to be counteracted by cold. Moreover, a full body desires (or loves) to be emptied, and vice versa. Of all the treatises in the Hippocratic corpus, Eryximachus' remarks are most similar to those in *On Regimen I*.

186e   *our ancestor Asclepius*: Eryximachus is claiming membership of the guild known as the Asclepiadae—'the descendants of Asclepius'. Asclepius was the legendary founder of the art of medicine; originally, the term 'Asclepiadae' referred to his literal sons, who played a part as doctors in the Trojan War, according to Homer. By the end of the fifth century the term was looser, and any doctor could claim to be descended from Asclepius.

186e   *poets like our friends here say*: Eryximachus points out Agathon and Aristophanes. It is not known which more ancient poets he is referring to, who might have discussed the foundation of medicine by Asclepius.

187a   *sport and agriculture*: because sport is concerned with bodies, agriculture with plants, and these were singled out in 186a as being governed by Love. On agriculture, see also Euripides, fragment 890 Nauck[2]: 'Under Aphrodite, the soil loves rain, the sky loves to rain. The intercourse between them engenders plants.'

187a   *a bow and a lyre*: Heraclitus, fragment 51 Diels–Kranz. Although the wording differs in different citations of the fragment, the meaning is plain enough: the tension which allows bows and lyres to exist and function is a principle in the universe at large. Eryximachus' criticism is hardly profound. The discussion by C. H. Kahn (in whose numbering it is fragment 78) is particularly good (*The Art and Thought of Heraclitus* (Cambridge: Cambridge University Press, 1979), 195–200).

187c   *Love's duality*: Eryximachus seems to be losing the thread. His talk promised to be an account of the duality of Love in all kinds of spheres, but he has boxed himself into a corner. He was so keen to show off by criticizing an authority as revered as Heraclitus that he has forced himself into a position where all music (even bad, discordant music) involves a relationship between the notes, and where relationship is the product of the good Love. Therefore, he cannot introduce discord as a parallel to sickness and a manifestation of bad Love in music.

187e   *the Muse Celestia*: this, in its Greek form Urania, was a recognized name of one of the Muses. Eryximachus suggests that the poetry she inspires is composed by moral people and can be used for morally sound education. However, the poetry inspired by Polymnia (which was also a recognized name, meaning 'the Muse of many songs') is ambiguous: it can lead an audience towards immorality. As sections of both *Republic* and *Laws* show as well, Plato was deeply concerned about the moral effects of poetry. Very few rhythms and modes (and very few subject-areas too) were acceptable to him. The same view is implicit here in the suspicion of Polymnia, the Muse of *many* songs.

187e *or a god*: such as Asclepius (186d–e).

188b *climatic conditions*: both the Greek sciences of *astronomia* and *meteorologia* could cover pretty much the same ground—the study of non-earthly phenomena.

189a *noises and tickles!*: this is a rather forced parody of elements of Eryximachus' speech (e.g. 186b). Despite the humour, however, it is not impossible that this is precisely what Eryximachus meant: if hiccuping is seen as taking in excess air, sneezing could be seen as expelling it and restoring the balance.

189b *interference*: the interference would come either from Eryximachus chuckling at *double entendres* he thought he had detected, since he was now in the mood to look out for jokes, or more particularly from his protests, since Aristophanes looks set to mock Eryximachus' speech.

189d *happened to it*: despite Aristophanes' fame as a comic poet, the fantasy that follows is Aesopic, aetiological folklore rather than learned comedy. The analysis by Dover (1966) of the antecedents of and echoes in Aristophanes' speech could hardly be bettered.

189e *as an insult*: it meant a coward, someone lacking in full manliness.

189e *forming a circle*: I follow the punctuation and interpretation of J. S. Morrison, 'Four Notes on Plato's *Symposium*', *Classical Quarterly*, 14 (1964), 42–55. The fifth-century philosopher Empedocles had also spoken of a former race of quasi-humans 'with faces and chests on both sides' (fragment 61 Diels–Kranz), but there is little resemblance to Aristophanes' theory, since for Empedocles these people were grotesque, not perfect: they were of the same species as creatures who were half-human, half-animal. Again, in fragment 62 Empedocles spoke of a former race of 'whole-natured beings', but they seem to be completely round, whereas Aristophanes' proto-humans have limbs.

190c *really about them*: see Homer, *Odyssey* 11. 307–20 (and the Index of Names under Ephialtes). In Homer's account, Ephialtes and Otus were huge giants, so Plato is having Aristophanes reinterpret Homer's story.

190e *with a hair*: it is possible to cut a hard-boiled egg in half with even a human hair (I've done it). The point of the comparison is that the matter was easy for Zeus: it takes no more than a hair to cut an egg, and it took Zeus hardly any effort to cut our ancestors in half.

191b *or of a male whole*: it would be pedantic to point out that Aristophanes has missed out surviving halves of androgynous wholes: we get the point.

191c *like cicadas*: it is not quite clear what Plato thinks cicadas get up to, but in any case he is wrong: they have perfectly normal sex.

191d *our counterparts*: turbots and other flat-fish, Plato suggests, look like rounded fish which have been sliced in half. A 'tally' (*sumbolon*) was half an item given by a host to a departing guest; the host retained the other half, to show that the guest would always be recognized and welcome back in his house.

191e *adulteresses*: since marriages were mostly arranged, rather than being love-matches, a sexually consummated love-affair would tend to involve adultery.

191e *from this group*: this is the only extant reference in classical Greek literature to female homosexuality.

192a *in government*: both politics and homosexuality were largely upper-class concerns. This aside rather awkwardly interrupts the sequence of thought (halves of all-male originals when they are boys . . . and when they are men . . .). Plato undoubtedly included it for the echo of the comic motif (e.g. Aristophanes' own *Clouds* 1088 ff.) of accusing public figures of homosexuality. Aristophanes' theorizing may also contain a caricature of medical views such as those in the Hippocratic treatise *On Regimen I*, 27 ff., where the virility of manly men is explained by their having gained a greater quantity of male parts from *both* their parents (and *mutatis mutandis* the femininity of feminine women is explained in the same way).

193a *pursuit of wholeness*: it adds to the sadness of Aristophanes' doctrine of unfulfilled and unfulfillable longing that he is the only one of the named protagonists of the dialogue who is alone. Phaedrus is with Eryximachus in some sense (176d, 177a ff., 223b, *Phaedrus* 268a), the affair between Pausanias and Agathon was notorious, and so in its own way was that between Socrates and Alcibiades.

193a *the Arcadians*: our knowledge of Arcadian history and the fluctuating relations between Arcadia and Sparta is so patchy that one hesitates to deny categorically that this could refer to some incident prior to the dramatic date of *Symposium* (416). Nevertheless, it remains the case that the most likely event took place in 385, when the Spartans razed the city of Mantinea in Arcadia and dispersed or 'scattered' the population. If this is the incident Plato is referring to, he is again (see note on 182b) being anachronistic; but anachronisms occur in nearly all his works. On the issue, see the articles by Mattingly and Dover (1965).

193a *half-dice*: dice were commonly used as tallies (see note on 191d).

194d *your contributions*: see 177c.

194e *my speech*: note the triple repetition of the phrase. This is a typical Gorgianic rhetorical flourish; see also the rhyme coming up between 'thrive' and 'contrive'. There will be many more at the end of Agathon's speech; see note on 197c.

195a *sacrilege and profanity*: he is anxious not to let his excessive praise of Love offend the other gods.

195b *Cronus and Iapetus*: see the Index of Names. Agathon chooses his ancient gods carefully, since in colloquial Greek to call someone a Cronus or an Iapetus was to suggest, in modern English slang, that he was 'well past his sell-by date'.

195c *castration and imprisonment*: we have no fragments of Parmenides on these events, but in his *Theogony* Hesiod recounts the story of Cronus' castration of his father Uranus, and of Zeus in his turn imprisoning his father Cronus.

195d *the lines*: Iliad 19. 92–3.

196a *making flowers his home*: this was a traditional poetic and artistic feature of portraits of Love. However, it is important to note that in Plato's time Love was not portrayed as the chubby, mischievous Cupid of later times, but as a fit, young, winged man. Note also that the Greek word *anthos* means both the 'bloom' of a flower and the 'bloom' or 'allure' of youth.

196c *law, society's king*: a *mot* attributed to Alcidamas, a fourth-century rhetorician who was a pupil of Gorgias.

196d *not even Ares can withstand Love*: Agathon paraphrases a line from Sophocles' lost play *Thyestes* (fragment 235 Nauck^2), changing 'Necessity' in the original to 'Love'.

196d *in the story*: the famous story told by Homer (*Odyssey* 8. 266 –366), of how Ares fell in love with Aphrodite, and they were caught in bed together by Aphrodite's husband Hephaestus.

196d *to discuss his wisdom*: these four make up a fairly standard list of what contemporary Greeks would have understood to constitute virtue or goodness, which is what Agathon is trying to attribute to Love.

196d *Eryximachus does his*: see 186b.

196e *however coarse he was before*: a snatch from Euripides' lost play *Sthenoboea* (fragment 666 Nauck^2).

197b *the captaincy of gods and men*: a fragment from an unknown poet, tentatively identified as Aeschylus by R. Renehan ('Three Places in Plato's *Symposium*', *Classical Philology*, 85 (1990), 125–6), on the grounds that Agathon's previous two quotations were from the other two of the triad of famous Athenian tragedians.

197b *love of beauty*: the relation between love and beauty is also developed in Socrates' speech. The reader should be aware from the start, however, that the Greek word *kalos* is impossible to translate identically in all contexts without awkwardness. It has been translated 'beautiful', 'attractive', or 'good-looking', chiefly, but in moral contexts it might mean 'good' or 'right'. See also note on 201c.

197c *those with cares*: we don't know where these two lines are from. Could Plato have lifted them from a work composed by the historical Agathon, or did he make them up himself, or did he quote them from some other author? Of the rhetorical features of Agathon's peroration, which immediately follows, some are obvious (the near-rhymes, the assonance, the asyndeton), but it should also be noted that in Greek it is also a mish-mash of poetic metres. This is reminiscent of the style of the famous sophist Gorgias of Leontini, as Socrates will point out at 198c. Gorgias also tended to structure his speeches as Agathon has—to start a paragraph by announcing the proposition to be demonstrated, then to demonstrate it, and finally to recapitulate. The other main sophistic feature in Agathon's speech is simply that he can produce arguments for obvious absurdities such as that love is self-controlled and love is never violent.

197d *festal, choral, sacrificial rites*: the three main forms of public, communal worship.

197d *gentle*: reading ἀγανός (Usener).

198c *turn me to stone*: Socrates alludes, in a somewhat laborious pun, to Homer, *Odyssey* 11. 634–5, where Odysseus flees the threat of the Gorgon (rather than Gorgias) whose gaze could turn people to stone. The words 'send', 'head', and 'formidable' are from Homer.

199a *not my heart*: Socrates paraphrases a notorious line Euripides puts into the mouth of Hippolytus: 'My tongue swore the oath, but my heart remains unsworn' (*Hippolytus* 612).

199b *words*: reading ὀνόμασι with the majority of the manuscripts.

199d *in this sense*: that is, in the sense 'born of', which is far more natural in Greek than in English.

201b *needs and lacks beauty*: from the fact that Love has love for beautiful *things*, nothing follows about whether or not Love is beautiful itself. The fallacy is equivocation on 'beauty', which either means the abstract concept beauty (which may be a property of Love or anyone else), or stands for 'all cases of beautiful things'. Agathon initially agrees that Love lacks beauty in this latter sense, and then Socrates illegitimately compels him to agree that Love lacks beauty in the former sense. Discussion of the passage can be found in R. E. Allen, 'A Note on the Elenchus of Agathon', *The Monist*, 50 (1966), 460–63; and in A. Soble, 'Love is Not Beautiful: *Symposium* 200e–201c', *Apeiron*, 19 (1985), 43–52. Still, fallacy apart, the meaning is plain: in so far as we are thinking of someone as in love, we do not need to take account of his or her attractiveness.

201c *also attractive*: the Greek word for 'attractive' (*kalos*) was a general term of commendation which could be used for moral qualities as much as for physical attributes or appropriateness or functional usefulness. But Plato is careful throughout his works never to identify the two qualities: to say that all good things are attractive or beautiful is not to say that all beautiful things are good. This becomes important in our dialogue in the sense that whereas Agathon is claiming that the object of love is beauty, Diotima later argues that it is goodness.

201c *lacks good qualities too*: remembering that the two chief claims in Agathon's speech have been that Love was attractive and good.

201d *for ten years*: the famous plague struck Athens in 430, so Plato is referring to an incident in 440 (the plague is described by the historian Thucydides (2. 47–54), but identification of the infection is uncertain). We have no way of knowing whether or not Diotima was a real person or a fictional creation of Plato's, and we have no other evidence that there was fear of the plague as early as 440. It is safest to record an open verdict on the issue of Diotima's historicity and the truth of this incident. Mantinea was a real town, however, in eastern Arcadia; if Diotima is a fiction, a pun is certainly intended, since *mantis* means 'diviner', and the point of this anecdote is to introduce her as a wandering seer, of the kind states called on during war or other emergencies. The 'itinerant charismatic who provides cures for various needs' (W. Burkert, *Ancient Mystery Cults* (Cambridge, Mass.: Harvard University Press, 1987), 43) was a familiar figure in the ancient Greek world: the best known are Epimenides of Crete, Apollonius of Tyana, and St Paul. They served a number of purposes, but commonly offered initiations, so neither the form (see p. xxviii) nor the content of Diotima's speech should come as a surprise.

202c *an enviable life*: all Greeks would have agreed that the gods have an enviable life, but their images of their gods were so thoroughly anthropomorphic that some gods *did* fall short of their notion of beauty (e.g. the crippled Hephaestus). But Diotima is a mouthpiece for Platonic ideas, and for Plato the concepts of badness and divinity were mutually exclusive.

203b *all the same*: Plotinus, the Neoplatonist of the third century AD, famously makes a great deal of Diotima's allegorical story in his essay on love (*Enneads* 3. 5).

203d *no shoes on his feet*: especially since, by 204a, Love and philosophy become more or less identified, we are bound to be reminded of Socrates' famous shoelessness (see 174a and 220b). Socrates is philosophy personified; later, of course, in Alcibiades' speech, he becomes Love personified as well.

204a *isn't aware of lacking*: in Greek, 'love of knowledge' is *philosophia*. If Love falls between knowledge and ignorance, and is therefore philosophy, we begin to see that Socrates' claim to be an expert on Love (177d, 198d) is not much different from his usual claim to know only that he is ignorant. Knowledge of ignorance is what impels a philosopher to try to gain knowledge, as Love does here. See also Plato's early dialogue *Lysis*, at 218b.

205a   *seems conclusive*: because 'happiness' (*eudaimonia*) was for a Greek by definition the ultimate purpose of life. It is what fulfils you, whatever you take that to be.

205c   *creators or poets*: Diotima's point in these two paragraphs is untranslatable in English. In Greek, the terms *poiēsis* and *poiētēs*, which basically just mean 'creativity' and 'creator', were usually reserved for 'poetry' and 'poet' (as in English 'artist' commonly means 'painter'). The same difficulty of translation arose at 187d and, more relevantly, at 196e–197a.

205d   *dominant, deceitful love*: the words are probably a paraphrase from a verse of poetry.

205d   *looking for their other halves*: this is, of course, an allusion to Aristophanes' speech, although Plato has Diotima speak in a vague way which allows him to maintain the fiction that Diotima is talking to Socrates long before the date of the (also fictional) symposium.

206b   *Love's purpose*: reading τούτου (Bast).

206b   *may be called love*: so now Diotima reverts to discussing the specific kind of love which we commonly call 'love', rather than the generic kind she has outlined. Even the specific kind must be love of goodness, of course, but this will manifest in a specific fashion.

206b   *in an attractive medium*: the Greek is literally 'procreation in something attractive'. The word 'in' should be taken at face value: the typical Greek attitude towards the female role in childbirth was that she was just a receptacle for the growth of the embryo, while all the properties of the child come from the father.

206c   *a kind of birth*: Plato wants to link the concepts of immortality and the attractiveness of beauty. In this paragraph, he achieves this by conflating human male–female sexual intercourse with childbirth. We need to be attracted to someone to have sex with him or her; the purpose of sexual intercourse is childbirth; childbirth is the closest we get to attaining immortality. The conflation is particularly striking later in the paragraph (206d–e), where Plato comes up with a single set of images to cover aspects of both sex and birth. For instance, the talk of relaxation is meant to encompass both the reaction of the female genitalia to sexual excitement and the dilation of the cervix at birth (and vice versa for the talk of contraction); the talk of swelling is meant to remind us not only of a heavily pregnant woman, but also of an erect penis. The conflation of sex and childbirth is further complicated by an additional conflation of gender: since procreation was commonly seen as a specifically female function in ancient Greece, Diotima is turning these male lovers into women. For discussion of the passage and further references, see E. E. Pender, 'Spiritual Pregnancy in Plato's *Symposium*', *Classical Quarterly*, 42 (1992), 72–86.

206d *at childbirth*: this is just to say that beauty is responsible for childbirth; see the Index of Names under Eileithyia.

206e *in a beautiful medium*: nevertheless, a great deal of emphasis continues to be placed on beauty as the object of love (especially at 210a–212a). But Diotima is not contradicting herself: she is driving a wedge between love's immediate, conscious object (which is beauty), and its long-term, subconscious object (which is procreation in a beautiful medium, as a means to happiness or possession of the good). The important distinction between conscious and subconscious desires first occurred in Aristophanes' speech (192c ff.).

207a *immortality as well*: it would be more natural to take the 'permanent' possession of goodness to mean possession throughout one's lifetime, and that is surely how the reader has been taking it since its introduction in 205a. We can forgive the fallacy, because of the importance of the insight that if our desires are limited to our own personal lifetimes, they take on a degree of futility. Once Diotima has understood 'permanence' as 'eternity', it is easy for her to unpack the desire as an implicit desire for immortality too. The introduction of eternity is helped not just by the general anticipatory nature of desire, but by the fact that Love has been shown to strive for things he does not have, and he was said at 202d to lack immortality.

208b *a body or whatever*: there is nothing here or in the previous paragraph which should lead us to think that at the time of writing *Symposium* Plato doubted the immortality of the human soul, or some part of it. This is a constant doctrine in other dialogues. In the previous paragraph, he is talking about low-level activities of the mind, which are particular to a given incarnation and therefore do not survive death; and in this paragraph he restricts himself to material objects, which are obviously perishable. To put this another way, in *Symposium* Plato is talking about the (necessarily limited) extent to which a specific person can be immortal, whereas in other dialogues he is talking about the immortality of souls (*psukhai*) which can, through reincarnation, be constituents of more than one person. Pythagoras may have been Euphorbus reincarnated, as he claimed, but that did not make him an identical person to Euphorbus.

208c *like a true sophist*: even though 'sophist' is invariably a term of insult in Plato, this phrase should not lead us to think that Plato doubted the value of Diotima's teaching. It is just that the sophists were notoriously—and often groundlessly—confident in the answers they gave. Some of them even made a display of inviting questions on *any* topic. So Diotima resembles a sophist only in being confident.

208c *fame immortal for ever*: the source of the line is unknown.

208d *joined Patroclus in death*: these were the two cases Phaedrus had made use of in his speech (179b–180b).

209c *education*: the emphasis here and in 210a–c on the educational aspect of a love-affair is supposed to remind us of Socrates' own conversations with young men, as immortalized in Plato's dialogues. The imagery of birth is bound to remind one of the famous metaphor of Socrates as a midwife of ideas in *Theaetetus* 148e–151d. The similarities and differences between the two passages are well discussed by M. F. Burnyeat, 'Socratic Midwifery, Platonic Inspiration', *Bulletin of the Institute of Classical Studies*, 24 (1977), 7–16, a paper which is reprinted in H. H. Benson (ed.), *Essays on the Philosophy of Socrates* (Oxford: Oxford University Press, 1992), 53–65.

209c *ordinary children*: here children are seen as the glue of a relationship, in such a way that the warmth and permanence of an affair may be measured by the degree of affection felt for the children. Since the offspring of the kind of relationship Plato is talking about are more attractive and more immortal, and since we feel love for that which is attractive and immortal, then we are bound to feel more love for such offspring, and therefore there will be more warmth and permanence in this

88

kind of relationship. It is relevant to remember the Athenian social context, that a man would not necessarily be expected to love his wife (the marriage would probably have been arranged), and yet she would be the one to bear his children: in such a situation, the bond of shared affection for children takes on great importance.

210a   *Watcher*: this was an advanced grade of initiation in both the Eleusinian and the Samothracian mysteries. However, in the case of both these mystery cults, the secret has been well kept, and we do not know quite what the Watchers saw or did. The most accessible recent discussion of the Greek mysteries in general can be found in W. Burkert, *Ancient Mystery Cults* (note on 201d).

210a   *his guide*: in the Eleusinian mysteries, the initiate would have been led by a guide—probably one of the officers known as Heralds—at certain stages. Outside the metaphor, the guide is perhaps Love (who makes a suitable herald, because he conveys messages etc. (202e–203a)), or perhaps the older partner in a relationship.

210e   *proper order and manner*: a central part of the Eleusinian mysteries was the unveiling of certain ritually significant objects before the celebrant's eyes.

211b   *entirely unaffected*: in expressing his conception of unchanging beauty, Plato not unnaturally drew on the vocabulary of the Presocratic philosopher-poet Parmenides, who claimed that in reality all is one and unchanging. See F. Solmsen, 'Parmenides and the Description of Perfect Beauty in Plato's *Symposium*', *American Journal of Philology*, 92 (1971), 62–70.

211b   *love for a boy*: we are reminded that male homoerotic love and 'mental' pregnancy have been the context all along. It is of course somewhat odd for Diotima—a woman—to be the expert in the higher mysteries of male homoerotic love. For an interesting discussion of this, and of other aspects of the dialogue which are concerned with sex and sexuality and reflect or reverse prevailing Athenian notions, see D. M. Halperin, 'Why is Diotima a Woman? Platonic Eros and the Figuration of Gender', in D. M. Halperin *et al.* (eds.), *Before Sexuality: The Construction of Erotic Experience in the Ancient Greek World* (Princeton, NJ: Princeton University Press, 1990), 257–308. Basically, he concludes, Diotima is a woman (or rather—since she is plainly a Socratic *alter ego*—

Socrates has to take on a female role) because women were considered the experts on reciprocity and on procreation.

211c *intellectual endeavour*: there are irresistible echoes in this paragraph of the upward ascent outlined in *Republic* 511b–c, which culminates in the vision of goodness, which is also called (e.g. at *Republic* 504d) the ultimate intellectual endeavour.

211c *so that*: reading ἵνα καὶ γνῷ (Usener, Bury).

212a *potential for immortality*: the only part of the mind which is immortal in itself is the intellect; the only mind or soul which is immortal as a whole is that which is wholly subservient to or one with the intellectual part. Again (see note on 208b) this is perfectly consistent with the doctrine of other dialogues.

212c *at one point*: 205d–e. See second note on 205d.

212c *pipe-girl's voice*: the immediate implication (see note on 176e) is that this is a slightly disreputable party. A street-party (*kōmos*) was held in celebration of some event and commonly involved a drunken procession through the streets—a pub-crawl would be the English equivalent. This one has stopped at a friend's house.

212e *over his head*: he is the very image of Dionysus. The way in which everyone enthusiastically invites him in (213a) shows how charming and popular Alcibiades was, and his 'sudden' appearance (212c) parallels the 'sudden' appearance of true beauty in Diotima's speech (210e). This is a dramatic expression of Alcibiades' famous good looks, but still to come is Socrates' 'sudden' appearance to Alcibiades on the couch (213b–c)—because ultimately Alcibiades' famous good looks pale into insignificance beside the kind of beauty Socrates bears within him.

212e *to that effect*: reading ἀνειπὼν οὑτωσί (Winckelmann).

213e *yesterday like you*: Socrates wins arguments, of course, rather than tragic competitions. A chaplet was a traditional prize for victory.

213e *your drinking*: see note on 176e. The 'agreement' Alcibiades refers to is that of 213a.

213e *big goblet*: a traditional feature of symposia, it was large enough to cater for the thirsts of all present, and it would be passed around from couch to couch.

213e *cooler*: one of the jars in which the wine for the whole evening would be kept. Wine was normally poured out of the cooler into a mixing-bowl, where it would be diluted with water before being served into the guests' cups. So Alcibiades is ensuring that the wine is drunk undiluted, as well as in incredibly large quantities. A *kotyle* is about half a pint, or about a quarter of a litre.

214b *many men*: Homer, *Iliad* 11. 514.

215a *for comic effect*: it was a common game in Athens for A to compare B to something ridiculous, and then for B to respond with an even more ridiculous image for A. So Alcibiades is guarding against the possibility that the others will think he is playing this game.

215b *look like these figures*: Sileni and Satyrs (for more information, see the Index of Names) were commonly portrayed in Greek art with a snub nose and bulging eyes, which we know (*Theaetetus* 143e) were familiar features of Socrates. See also Xenophon, *Symposium* 4. 19.

215b *brutally*: the 'brutality' for which Silenus and other Satyrs were notorious was drunken rape (they were usually depicted on vases with huge erections, and often in pursuit of some victim); so the Greek word can mean just 'rape'. Socrates was also accused of brutality by Agathon at 175e (and his merciless ways with his interlocutors are remarked on several times in other Platonic dialogues). But when Alcibiades accuses Socrates of Silenus-like brutality in his speech (here and at 219c and 222a) there is a joke: despite refusing to have sex with him, Socrates 'raped' him.

215c *Olympus' teacher*: see the Index of Names for Marsyas and Olympus. Alcibiades is referring to the fact that different legends accredited them both with the invention of the *aulos* (see note on 176e).

215c *ready for initiation*: the audience, already primed by the mystery-cult imagery of Diotima's speech, would be bearing in mind that the Satyrs and Sileni were not only the coarse figures of ribald imagination, but were commonly depicted also as the priests of the Dionysiac mysteries. The Dionysiac and Eleusinian mysteries were not as distinct as the existence of the two names might suggest; so if Socrates is a priest of the mysteries, he has taken the place of the priestess Diotima.

215e   *the Corybantes*: a mystical group, originating in Anatolia, whose practices included pipe-playing and shamanistic drumming to attain ecstasy and union with the Great Goddess.

216c   *sadness*: strangely, this mixture of love and loathing is *exactly* the reaction even contemporary reporters (Aristophanes, *Frogs* 1425), let alone later commentators (e.g. Plutarch, *Life of Alcibiades*), attributed to Athens about Alcibiades himself. And regret is what Plato thinks Athens should feel at having killed Socrates (*Apology* 39c). Alcibiades—brilliant but flawed— here represents Athens: he is crowned with violets (212e), and there was an ode of Pindar's (which was as famous in Athens as a national anthem is in a modern country), which uniquely described Athens as crowned in violets (Pindar, fragment 76 Snell).

216d   *how Silenus-like he looks*: a Silenus would be in a stupor of drunken ignorance. The *locus classicus* for Socrates' 'stupor' at the sight of a good-looking young man is his encounter with Charmides at the beginning of Plato's dialogue *Charmides* (154b–155e), and an erotic element is very common in Plato's early dialogues.

217c   *get me somewhere*: especially since it was usual to exercise naked.

217e   *slaves into consideration*: there is a joke here. The original proverb ran, 'Truth comes from wine and children.' But since the word for children (*paides*) also means 'slaves' (as slaves in the southern states of America used to be referred to as 'boys'), then Alcibiades is saying, first, 'whether or not I take children into consideration', and at the same time, 'whether or not I take into consideration the fact that there are slaves present here who might inhibit my speech' (see 218b).

218b   *non-initiates here*: yet another nod in the direction of the mystery cults, and also a parody of the movement in Diotima's speech from a lower to a less attainable grade of initiation (209e–210a).

218c   *anything else you want*: notice the echo of Pausanias' idea at 184c ff.

219a   *gold for bronze*: a snatch from Homer, *Iliad* 6. 236, which had become proverbial. In the original poem, Glaucus suffers a fit of stupidity and swaps his golden armour for Diomedes' bronze armour.

219a *goes into decline*: reading [λήγειν] ἀποχωρῇ (Waterfield).

219b *his short cloak*: Socrates was notoriously impervious to the weather. Although at 220a–b we do hear of him wearing a *himation* (a thicker, longer outer garment) in extreme weather conditions, in Athens he wore only a *tribōn* (a short, thin outer garment for summer) all the year round. As already mentioned (note on 203d), he generally wore no shoes either. Later, this style of his became the badge of a philosopher. It was quite normal to use your outer garment as a blanket during the night, and sleep in your under-garments: Alcibiades and Socrates were not naked together this time!

219c *prided myself on*: Alcibiades was in fact considered the best-looking man in Athens of his generation (*Protagoras* 309c).

219e *at Potidaea*: in 432 war against Sparta had become inevitable. Corinth was Sparta's ally; Potidaea, which had links with both Athens and Corinth and was strategically placed to govern sea-routes in the northern Aegean, refused to accede to Athenian demands to come fully over to their side. The Athenians besieged the city for two years before it surrendered.

220a *Socrates drunk*: this repeated theme (see also 176c, 214a and 223c–d) is also symbolized by the fact that Socrates is as impervious to Alcibiades' charms as he is to wine, and Alcibiades is a Dionysiac figure (see note on 212e). Since Socrates is Love personified (simply because he takes the place of Love in Alcibiades' encomium), the point is that Love can be impervious to Dionysus: Love need not be ecstatic frenzy, as Diotima showed (and Plato's *Phaedrus* confirms).

220c *man performed*: Homer, *Odyssey* 4. 242 or 271, slightly altered to fit the context better (as is Plato's common practice).

220e *as well as my life*: it was important to keep your weapons and armour safe, to avoid charges of having abandoned them through cowardice; see 179a.

220e *the prize for valour*: it consisted of an olive wreath. Only one was awarded per battle: it was a kind of competition, to encourage bravery.

221a *from Delium*: in 424, Athens invaded Boeotia and established a garrison at Delium. The main army was on its way back to Athens when it was routed by the Boeotians. Socrates' part in the battle is also mentioned at *Laches* 181b.

221a *hoplite*: heavy infantry. Since hoplites (like cavalrymen) provided their own equipment, and it was expensive, Athenians were assigned to these battalions as a result of a property assessment. This gives the lie to the tradition of Socrates' poverty, which sprang up soon after his death. He came from a well-to-do middle-class background, although he adopted an ascetic life-style and clearly had no interest in making money.

221b *eyes alert*: a version of Aristophanes' description of Socrates' mannerisms at *Clouds* 362.

221e *brutal Satyr's skin*: this is subtle. At first sight, it says no more than it appears to—Socrates' arguments are like a Silenus because they too have an outer surface. However, the most famous Satyr's skin was that of Marsyas himself, who was flayed alive and turned into a wineskin (see the Index of Names). But the Greek for wineskin (*askos*) was also the slang for 'windbag'. So Alcibiades is implying that when you first hear Socrates arguing, you might think he is just an old windbag.

221e *shoe-makers, tanners*: we very commonly find Socrates, both in the early Platonic dialogues and in Xenophon's records of Socratic conversations, inferring that what goes for two or three branches of expertise goes for all branches of expertise —and especially expertise at living, which is virtue or goodness. This 'Craft Analogy' is the origin of the famous Socratic paradox that 'Virtue is knowledge'.

222b *before understanding it*: there are allusions to this proverb from the very earliest Greek literature (e.g. Homer, *Iliad* 17. 32).

222c *sober, I think*: Socrates refers to Alcibiades' words at 213e.

222d *Silenus-like play-acting of yours*: it is 'Satyrical' (the pun captures Plato's tone) and 'Silenus-like' because it conceals one thing inside another, as in Alcibiades' own speech.

222e *lie between us*: is it too far-fetched to see here the tussle between two ways of life? Socrates is the detached philosopher, Alcibiades the politician, immersed in the world. Agathon represents goodness—we remember the pun on his name (174b)—and chooses Socrates' side.

222e *on my right*: a humorous conflation of 177d and 214c.

223b *completely unsystematic*: democratic presidency (see note on 176e) gave way to Alcibiades' tyranny (213e–214a), but there was still some order to his presidency; now, however, there is complete anarchy, though order is restored by dawn (223c).

223d *comic playwright*: in classical times, no playwright wrote both tragedies and comedies, though tragedians also wrote Satyr-plays (see Index of Names under Silenus). We will never know what Socrates' argument might have been (it would have to have contradicted *Republic* 395a), but note that his audience consists of Agathon the tragedian and Aristophanes the comedian. It has been suggested that Plato is commenting obliquely on the presence of both the solemnity of tragedy and the burlesque of comedy in *Symposium*. The main manifestation of this is in the contrast between Diotima's and Alcibiades' roles, but it is also worth noting how Plato has the comedian Aristophanes tell a tragic tale of man's original sin and its consequences, and the tragedian Agathon give a speech which is not meant to be wholly serious (197e); and then see also p. xl. So perhaps, among other things, Plato means us to think of himself as the one who combines the skills of tragic and comic playwright.

223d *the Lyceum*: a gymnasium and public baths.

INDEX OF NAMES

Achilles: the supreme warrior on the Greek side in HOMER's *Iliad*.
After quarrelling with AGAMEMNON over an issue of status, he
withdraws from the battle against the Trojans. It is only the death
of his friend PATROCLUS that galvanizes him back into action.

Acusilaus: a little-known sixth-century genealogist/historian from
Argos; one of the earliest writers to write in prose.

Admetus: see ALCESTIS.

Aeschylus: *c.*525–456, the earliest of the three outstanding Athenian
tragic playwrights, he established the basic forms of classical
tragedy.

Agamemnon: the leader of the Greek forces at the legendary siege of
Troy, a few episodes of which are dramatically told in HOMER's
Iliad.

Agathon: born *c.*445. In his time, he was a highly regarded tragic
playwright, though only a few lines of his work are extant now. He
was famous as a modernizer (e.g. for not drawing his plots from
myth and for not integrating his choral odes with the plots of his
plays), for his somewhat overblown poetry, for his physical beauty,
for his affair with PAUSANIAS, and for having been influenced by
the sophistic movement (as is painfully evident in his speech in our
dialogue). He left Athens in 407 and emigrated to the court of King
Archelaus of Macedon, who was a great patron of the arts.

Ajax: in HOMER's *Iliad*, Ajax is not just an outstanding warrior,
like most of the heroes, but carries a huge shield, so that he is
particularly hard to wound.

Alcestis: a famous heroine from legend. Her husband Admetus forgot
to sacrifice to Artemis at their wedding, for which the punishment
was death—unless someone would die in his place. Alcestis offered
to do just this. She died, but after her death she was allowed to
come back to life. There are various versions of the story, the most
famous of which, for us, is that of Euripides' *Alcestis*.

Alcibiades: 452–404. As a young man in Athens, Alcibiades showed
extraordinary promise as a politician and military strategist, and
the Athenians adored him. He had immense personal charisma and
wealth; he came from a noble family and was brought up after his
father's death by no less a person than the undisputed leader of
Athens, PERICLES. He squandered all this talent and opportunity,
however, by his scandalous personal behaviour and oligarchic

97

political associations. In 415 (a year after the setting of *Symposium*), when he was about to take command of Athens' do-or-die military expedition to Sicily, he was exiled; the immediate reason was his alleged involvement in parodying the sacred Eleusinian mysteries in the presence of non-initiates, and in the sacrilegious mutilation of statues of Hermes all over Athens (the statues were ithyphallic and had their phalluses broken off). For several years he helped Athens' enemies, before becoming a kind of overlord in Thrace and allying himself once again with Athens. This led to his reinstatement in Athens in 407, but it was short-lived and he fled to his northern territories. He was assassinated in 404 by agents of the Persian king. In biographical tradition (Plutarch's *Life of Alcibiades* is particularly good), he became the type of the wayward genius with the ability to adapt himself to his surroundings. Socrates was said to be the only person who could control him at all.

Antenor: the Trojan counterpart to Greek NESTOR.

Aphrodite: the goddess of attraction and sexual love (originally of fertility); married to HEPHAESTUS and lover of ARES. See also note on 180e.

Apollo: the god of archery, healing, music, reason, and prophecy.

Apollodorus: the narrator of the whole dialogue. All we know about him comes from the Socratic works of Plato and Xenophon. He was a devoted follower of Socrates; see further note on 173d.

Ares: the god of the frenzy of war. He fell for APHRODITE's charms and they had a notorious affair which ended when Aphrodite's husband HEPHAESTUS ensnared them *in flagrante delicto* in a magic net he had made and summoned all the rest of the gods to come and look.

Aristodemus: the main source of the story of the symposium, at which he himself was present. Hardly anything is known about him; see note on 173b.

Aristogiton: see HARMODIUS.

Aristophanes: *c*.450–*c*.385. The greatest playwright of Athenian Old Comedy, notorious for its slapstick obsessions with sex, food, alcohol, farting, and belching. It was also a powerful tool of social and political satire—no public figure was safe (Socrates himself is unfairly parodied in the *Clouds*, as is AGATHON in *Thesmophoriazousae*). His speech in our dialogue approximates to his plays only in the element of the fantastic.

Asclepius: in HOMER, he is a human being who founded the art of medicine, but he soon became elevated to the ranks of divinity with his own cult as a god of healing. His cult involved not just irrational features, like healing by dream-interpretation, but also practical curatives such as diet and regimen. So the rising class of professional physicians like ERYXIMACHUS could justly claim descent from him, even though they were trying to put their work on a far more scientific basis.

Athena: the patron goddess of Athens, and the goddess of skill at war and of traditionally female skills, especially weaving.

Brasidas: an outstanding Spartan commander during the Peloponnesian War between Athens and Sparta (431–404). He was killed in 422. It is his personal bravery which earns him the comparison with ACHILLES (221c).

Celestia: a Muse—i.e. an inspirer and patron of artistic works.

Charmides: a good-looking young Athenian aristocrat who was a member of Socrates' circle. He was Plato's uncle, and one of Plato's early dialogues is named after him. He sided with the brutal oligarchs who took control of Athens with Spartan support in 404, and died fighting against the democratic counter-revolution of 403.

Codrus: a legendary early king of Athens. During his reign, the Delphic oracle told the Dorians that they could invade Attica (the district around Athens) and that they would be successful if they kept Codrus alive. Codrus heard of this, disguised himself as a woodcutter and went out to meet the Dorians. He picked a quarrel with some of them and was killed—thus thwarting the invasion and preserving his dynasty for another three hundred years.

Cronus: after deposing his father URANUS, he became king of the gods, until he in turn was deposed by his son ZEUS. The tales are told in HESIOD's *Theogony*.

Dione: a minor goddess whose chief claim to fame in historical times was that, in one version of the myth of APHRODITE's birth, she was her mother by ZEUS.

Dionysus: the god of liberation. On more refined levels, this meant liberation through emotional, and especially ecstatic, rites. On a debased level, it meant liberation through getting drunk.

Diotima: though the name is attested elsewhere, she is probably a fiction of Plato's for the purpose of the dialogue. Even if she is, or is based on, a historical figure, she has become in the dialogue a mouthpiece for Platonic doctrine. As such, she allows Socrates to show up the superficiality of his friends' speeches in a polite manner appropriate to the context, and to exhibit his question-and-answer technique while pretending to obey the rules of the contest and give a speech. Since there is a delicious ambiguity whether the *intellectual* side of Love's mysteries is all that she initiated Socrates into, it is tempting to see her as one of those educated courtesans whose prime historical example is Aspasia (common-law wife of PERICLES). Her primary model, however, is that of the itinerant mystic: see note on 201d.

Eileithyia: the goddess whose job it was to oversee childbirth, where one or more of the personified Fates would also have been present to seal the child's fate.

Ephialtes: a giant in mythology who, with his companion Otus, was notoriously hostile to the rule of the Olympic pantheon. Their most famous escapade was to launch an attack on heaven by piling mount Ossa on top of mount Olympus (high above which was the abode of the gods), and then Pelion on top of Ossa.

Eryximachus: one of the new professional doctors of the end of the fifth century, who was obviously well known in Athenian intellectual circles, since he crops up from time to time in other Socratic writings of Plato and Xenophon.

Euripides: c.485–406, the third (with Sophocles and AESCHYLUS) of the three great Athenian tragic playwrights. Although based on ancient myths, his plays are more 'modern' and psychological than those of the other two.

Euthydemus: not to be confused with the sophist Euthydemus of Chios, after whom one of Plato's dialogues is named, this Euthydemus of Athens is unknown outside his enshrinement in the Socratic writings of Plato and Xenophon and later Socratic legend as a good-looking young man whom Socrates attracted towards philosophy.

Glaucon: a friend of APOLLODORUS. Glaucon was a common name in Plato's family: his brother of that name is an interlocutor in Republic and also occurs in Xenophon's Memorabilia, and CHARMIDES' father of that name was Plato's great-uncle. But we are not given enough information about the Glaucon of 172c to know who he was.

Gorgias: c.480–376, from Leontini in Sicily. One of the outstanding figures of the sophistic movement, and a well-known figure in Athens. He specialized not in philosophy, but in the budding art of rhetoric, in which he was a great innovator; although much of his style seems horribly artificial to us today, it seems to have dazzled his contemporaries. 'Starting with the initial advantage of having nothing in particular to say, he was able to concentrate all his energies upon saying it' (J. D. Denniston, Greek Prose Style (London: Oxford University Press, 1952), 12).

Harmodius: he and Aristogiton were famed in Athens as 'the tyrannicides'. From 527 to 510 Athens was ruled by a tyrant called

Hippias. In 514, Harmodius and Aristogiton planned to assassinate both Hippias and his brother Hipparchus. They succeeded only in killing Hipparchus, however, and were caught and killed themselves by Hippias. After Hippias had been overthrown, they became popular Athenian heroes and figures of sculpture. The Athenians conveniently forgot that their motives were perhaps not primarily political: they were lovers and wanted to get rid of Hipparchus because he was persistently trying to seduce Harmodius.

Hector: the supreme warrior on the Trojan side in HOMER's *Iliad*. It is the death of PATROCLUS at his hands that spurs ACHILLES back into action.

Hephaestus: the lame smith of the Olympic pantheon (originally with all the magical connotations that accrue to smiths the world over). In one tradition, mankind was his creation: this, as well as his role as metal-worker, probably underlies his role in ARISTOPHANES' speech.

Heracles: the great hero of Greek legend, famous for his twelve labours and an important figure in numerous other stories. He also had a thriving cult throughout Greece.

Heraclitus: *c*.540–*c*.480, from Ephesus in Asia Minor, an enigmatic philosopher-prophet, much given to aphorisms, who was particularly famous for trying to alert people to the impermanence of things.

Hesiod: fl. *c*.700, he was considered by the Greeks their second greatest epic poet (after HOMER). His *Theogony* orders the gods into rationalistic genealogies and recounts stories about many of them, while *Works and Days* is full of practical and moral advice for rural everyday life. Other poems are more or less lost.

Homer: fl. *c*.750, the greatest epic poet of Greece. His *Iliad* sings of death and glory in the legendary Trojan War, while his *Odyssey* tells of the fantastic adventures of one of the Greek heroes, Odysseus, during his voyage home after the war.

Iapetus: a mythical Titan, brother to CRONUS, and defeated with him by ZEUS. Since Zeus represents the current world-order, Cronus and Iapetus stand for the past.

Laches: an Athenian military commander during the Peloponnesian War, and a friend of Socrates. One of Plato's early dialogues, on courage, is named after him. He died at the battle of Mantinea in 418.

Lycurgus: a semi-legendary Spartan, who was acclaimed as the founder of their constitution. Since he was traditionally dated to the eighth or even the tenth century BC, he was one of the earliest

Greek law-makers, and therefore may be said (as at 209d) to have helped all of Greece, not merely Sparta.

Marsyas: a mythical SATYR who was famous as a musician. He was often credited with the invention of the *aulos* (reed-pipe) or at least with considerable and innovatory expertise in it. In fact, the most famous story about him has him challenging APOLLO and his lyre to a musical competition: the winner could do what he wanted with the loser. Apollo won, of course, flayed Marsyas alive and turned him into a wineskin. It is best not to challenge the gods!

Melanippe: a mythical person whose shadowy status is not helped by the loss of Euripides' two plays about her. This Melanippe is probably the daughter of Chiron, seduced by Aeolus the god of the winds and later transformed into a mare (rather than the one who was the daughter of Aeolus and bore Poseidon two fine calves).

Menelaus: AGAMEMNON's brother, but generally acknowledged to be a much softer person than his brother. It was the theft by Paris of Troy of Menelaus' wife Helen that initiated the Trojan War.

Nestor: in HOMER, Nestor is a somewhat loquacious old man, whose part in the Trojan War is as an adviser and speaker. When Plato compares him to PERICLES, then, it is Pericles' gifts as a statesman that he is thinking of.

Olympus: a mythical associate of MARSYAS who is credited with the same musical inventions and innovations.

Orpheus: the famous legendary bard and eponymous founder of an obscure branch of Greek mysticism. Of the many stories about him, the ones to which Plato refers in 179d are as follows. First, he tried to rescue his dead wife Eurydice from the underworld; in the usual version, however, Eurydice was not a 'phantom', but Orpheus turned back to look at her as she followed him out of Hades, whereupon she was taken back down. And second, he was torn to pieces (quite why is unclear) by maenads or female followers of DIONYSUS from his native Thrace.

Otus: see EPHIALTES.

Parmenides: *c.*515–*c.*440, from Elea in southern Italy, a metaphysical philosopher of astonishing profundity, famous for proposing that in reality everything was one and unchanging. He also entered into the mainstream of Presocratic cosmogonical debate, and this is the context of his mention in 178b and 195c; however, we know little of his cosmogonical views.

Patroclus: in HOMER's *Iliad*, the close friend of ACHILLES.

Pausanias: scarcely known apart from this dialogue, and chiefly known as AGATHON's lover. This probably explains his entry into our dialogue, where he is the champion of homosexuality—a rather outspoken champion, to judge by Xenophon's criticism in his own *Symposium* (8. 32–4).

Pericles: *c.*495–429, an outstanding statesman and the virtual ruler of supposedly democratic Athens from about 450 until his death from the plague.

Phaedrus: a minor Socratic and a recurrent figure in Plato's dialogues (one of which is named after him and is also concerned with love). The year after the setting of our dialogue, Phaedrus was exiled for complicity in the same scandal that caused ALCIBIADES' exile, and he only returned under the general amnesty at the end of the war.

Phoenix: utterly unknown apart from his incidental mention at 172b, from which we may tentatively infer that he was a member of Socrates' circle.

Polymnia: a Muse—i.e. an inspirer and patron of artistic works.

Prodicus: a contemporary of Socrates from the island of Ceos and one of the leading lights of the sophistic movement.

Satyrs: mischievous and sometimes worse than mischievous Pan-like nature spirits, who because of their libertine and erotic nature became associated with DIONYSUS in his lower form. They were portrayed as pot-bellied, snub-nosed, and bulge-eyed (see note on 215b), and often with prominent erections. Traditionally, they are half-man, half-goat.

Silenus: originally the name of a follower or possibly teacher of DIONYSUS, and perhaps the original SATYR, but his name became pluralized and more or less synonymous with 'Satyrs'. Like MARSYAS, he was associated with music and especially the *aulos*. In Athens he was particularly famous as a recurrent figure in the Satyr-plays, which were parodies of Greek myths, written by the tragedians and put on along with their tragedies at the dramatic festivals. At a less coarse level, however, Silenus appears as the chief priest of the Dionysiac mysteries. No example of the kind of figurine to which ALCIBIADES likens Socrates and his conversations in his speech has survived.

Sirens: wicked women whose charming singing lured sailors to their death. Their most famous appearance is in HOMER's *Odyssey* 12, where Odysseus blocks up his men's ears, and has himself tied to the ship's mast, so that he can hear the Sirens without endangering his ship and crew.

Solon: fl. *c.*590, a famous Athenian statesman and lyric poet. He is one of the constant members of the varying lists of the Seven Sages of Greece, and was regarded in Athenian popular history as the founding father of their democracy.

Uranus: his name means 'Sky' or 'Heaven' and he was seen as a primordial deity, who founded the lineage of gods by mating with Earth. His rulership was ended by a rebellion of his son CRONUS and the other Titans.

Zeus: the undisputed king of the pantheon of gods who occupied Olympus.

THE WORLD'S CLASSICS

A Select List

HANS ANDERSEN: Fairy Tales
Translated by L. W. Kingsland
Introduction by Naomi Lewis
Illustrated by Vilhelm Pedersen and Lorenz Frølich

LUDOVICO ARIOSTO: Orlando Furioso
Translated by Guido Waldman

ARISTOTLE: The Nicomachean Ethics
Translated by David Ross

JANE AUSTEN: Emma
Edited by James Kinsley and David Lodge

HONORÉ DE BALZAC: Père Goriot
Translated and Edited by A. J. Krailsheimer

CHARLES BAUDELAIRE: The Flowers of Evil
Translated by James McGowan
Introduction by Jonathan Culler

R. D. BLACKMORE: Lorna Doone
Edited by Sally Shuttleworth

MARY ELIZABETH BRADDON: Lady Audley's Secret
Edited by David Skilton

CHARLOTTE BRONTË: Jane Eyre
Edited by Margaret Smith

EMILY BRONTË: Wuthering Heights
Edited by Ian Jack

GEORG BÜCHNER:
Danton's Death, Leonce and Lena, Woyzeck
Translated by Victor Price

JOHN BUNYAN: The Pilgrim's Progress
Edited by N. H. Keeble

FRANCES HODGSON BURNETT: The Secret Garden
Edited by Dennis Butts

LEWIS CARROLL: Alice's Adventures in Wonderland
and Through the Looking Glass
Edited by Roger Lancelyn Green
Illustrated by John Tenniel

MIGUEL DE CERVANTES: Don Quixote
Translated by Charles Jarvis
Edited by E. C. Riley

GEOFFREY CHAUCER: The Canterbury Tales
Translated by David Wright

ANTON CHEKHOV: The Russian Master and Other Stories
Translated by Ronald Hingley

Ward Number Six and Other Stories
Translated by Ronald Hingley

WILKIE COLLINS: Armadale
Edited by Catherine Peters

No Name
Edited by Virginia Blain

JOSEPH CONRAD: Chance
Edited by Martin Ray

Lord Jim
Edited by John Batchelor

Youth, Heart of Darkness, The End of the Tether
Edited by Robert Kimbrough

THOMAS DE QUINCEY:
The Confessions of an English Opium-Eater
Edited by Grevel Lindop

STENDHAL: The Red and the Black
Translated by Catherine Slater

TOBIAS SMOLLETT: The Expedition of Humphry Clinker
Edited by Lewis M. Knapp
Revised by Paul-Gabriel Boucé

ROBERT LOUIS STEVENSON: Kidnapped and Catriona
Edited by Emma Letley

Treasure Island
Edited by Emma Letley

BRAM STOKER: Dracula
Edited by A. N. Wilson

JONATHAN SWIFT: Gulliver's Travels
Edited by Paul Turner

WILLIAM MAKEPEACE THACKERAY: Barry Lyndon
Edited by Andrew Sanders

LEO TOLSTOY: Anna Karenina
Translated by Louise and Aylmer Maude
Introduction by John Bayley

War and Peace
Translated by Louise and Aylmer Maude
Edited by Henry Gifford

ANTHONY TROLLOPE: The American Senator
Edited by John Halperin

Dr. Thorne
Edited by David Skilton

Dr. Wortle's School
Edited by John Halperin

Orley Farm
Edited by David Skilton

IVAN TURGENEV: First Love and Other Stories
Translated by Richard Freeborn

MARK TWAIN: Pudd'nhead Wilson and Other Tales
Edited by R. D. Gooder

GIORGIO VASARI: The Lives of the Artists
Translated and Edited by Julia Conaway Bondanella and Peter Bondanella

JULES VERNE: Journey to the Centre of the Earth
Translated and Edited by William Butcher

VIRGIL: The Aeneid
Translated by C. Day Lewis
Edited by Jasper Griffin

The Eclogues and The Georgics
Translated by C. Day Lewis
Edited by R. O. A. M. Lyne

HORACE WALPOLE: The Castle of Otranto
Edited by W. S. Lewis

IZAAK WALTON and CHARLES COTTON:
The Compleat Angler
Edited by John Buxton
Introduction by John Buchan

OSCAR WILDE: Complete Shorter Fiction
Edited by Isobel Murray

The Picture of Dorian Gray
Edited by Isobel Murray

MARY WOLLSTONECRAFT:
Mary *and* The Wrongs of Woman
Edited by Gary Kelly

VIRGINIA WOOLF: Mrs Dalloway
Edited by Claire Tomalin

ÉMILE ZOLA:
The Attack on the Mill and Other Stories
Translated by Douglas Parmée

Nana
Translated and Edited by Douglas Parmée

A complete list of Oxford Paperbacks, including The World's Classics, OPUS, Past Masters, Oxford Authors, Oxford Shakespeare, and Oxford Paperback Reference, is available in the UK from the Arts and Reference Publicity Department (BH), Oxford University Press, Walton Street, Oxford OX2 6DP.

In the USA, complete lists are available from the Paperbacks Marketing Manager, Oxford University Press, 200 Madison Avenue, New York, NY 10016.

Oxford Paperbacks are available from all good bookshops. In case of difficulty, customers in the UK can order direct from Oxford University Press Bookshop, Freepost, 116 High Street, Oxford, OX1 4BR, enclosing full payment. Please add 10 per cent of published price for postage and packing.